# Digital Youth with Disabilities

**The John D. and Catherine T. MacArthur Foundation Reports on Digital Media and Learning**

A complete series list can be found at the back of the book.

# Digital Youth with Disabilities

Meryl Alper

The MIT Press
Cambridge, Massachusetts
London, England

MIT Press books may be purchased at special quantity discounts for business or sales promotional use. For information, please email special_sales@mitpress.mit.edu.

This book was set in Stone by the MIT Press. Printed and bound in the United States of America.

Library of Congress Cataloging-in-Publication Data

Alper, Meryl.
Digital youth with disabilities / Meryl Alper.
    page   cm. — (The John D. and Catherine T. MacArthur Foundation reports on digital media and learning)
Includes bibliographical references.
ISBN 978-0-262-52715-6 (pbk. : alk. paper)
1. Mass media and youth—United States. 2. Digital media—Social aspects—United States. 3. Youth with disabilities—United States. 4. Technology and youth—United States. I. Title.
HQ799.2.M352U647   2015
305.9′08083—dc23
2014017230

10   9   8   7   6   5   4   3   2   1

# Contents

## Series Foreword

The John D. and Catherine T. MacArthur Foundation Reports on Digital Media and Learning, published by the MIT Press in collaboration with the Monterey Institute for Technology and Education (MITE), present findings from current research on how young people learn, play, socialize, and participate in civic life. The reports result from research projects funded by the MacArthur Foundation as part of its fifty million dollar initiative in digital media and learning. They are published openly online (as well as in print) in order to support broad dissemination and stimulate further research in the field.

# Acknowledgments

I would like to thank Ellen Seiter, my dissertation committee member and editor of the John D. and Catherine T. MacArthur Foundation Reports on Digital Media and Learning series, for her guidance and advice on this project. I also appreciate the continued support of the Annenberg School for Communication and Journalism at the University of Southern California, especially my primary doctoral studies adviser, Henry Jenkins. I am extremely grateful for the insights shared with me by the youth and adults with disabilities who I have met over the course of my research as well as their families, friends, teachers, and supporters. In addition, I would like to thank the following individuals for being invaluable thought partners as I worked through the ideas in this report: Mike Ananny, François Bar, Elizabeth Ellcessor, Beth Haller, Sara Hendren, Paul Lichterman, Melissa Morgenlander, Mara Mills, and Rachel Proffitt. Lastly, I wish to thank Susan Buckley at the MIT Press and the anonymous outside readers for their feedback on the manuscript.

# 1 Introduction

This report synthesizes the existing scholarship, and suggests future areas for research on the various roles that media and technology play in the lives of school-age youth with disabilities (three to twenty-two years old) and their families in the United States, with a focus on media use at home and as part of household activities.[1] It has three main aims: to summarize how children with disabilities take up media for social and recreational purposes; to reframe common assumptions about the relationships (both positive and negative) between children with disabilities and information and communication technologies; and to identify areas for further inquiry into the role of new media in the lives of children with disabilities, parents, and caregivers. This book outlines the parameters of research on digital youth with disabilities, and calls for more investigation as well as better translation of research into practice.

Disability is central to the human experience. At one time or another, those of us who are "temporarily able-bodied" will become disabled, whether as part of the aging process or unexpectedly at any age. People with disabilities have the same human rights to live with dignity and self-worth as those without disabilities. Yet significant cultural, technological, political,

and economic barriers continue to limit the full societal participation of children and adults with disabilities in the digital age
(Dobransky and Hargittai 2006; Ellcessor 2010). Only 54 percent
of adults with disabilities in the United States report that they
use the Internet, compared with 81 percent of adults without
disabilities (Fox 2011). Fewer households headed by someone
with a disability in the United States report owning a computer
(53 percent) than do all US households (76 percent) (US Department of Commerce 2013). Lack of Internet connectivity impacts
the extent to which individuals with disabilities can seek health
information, find employment, learn about events in the world,
and enjoy all the ordinary, mundane, and everyday activities
that people do online. It is not just individuals with disabilities
and their families who are impacted by this exclusion but also
society writ large, which loses out on their contributions.

Contrary to popular claims, new media are not inherently
"equalizers" for people with disabilities (Borchert 1998), just as
the Internet is not innately liberating. The greater (though not
fully realized) social and digital inclusion of people with disabilities in recent decades is largely due to a number of major social,
cultural, and political shifts in the United States. The end of
the twentieth century marked the hard-earned passage of land-
mark civil rights legislation, most notably the Rehabilitation Act
of 1973, Education for All Handicapped Children Act in 1975
(amended in 1990 by the Individuals with Disabilities Education
Act, or IDEA), Americans with Disabilities Act (ADA) in 1990,
and Assistive Technology Act of 2004. The disability rights and
independent living movements have fought—and continue to
do so—for self-determination, self-respect, and self-representation for people with disabilities (Shapiro 1993).

For youth with disabilities, federal legislation ostensibly ensures their right to technology and related services as needed to access school curriculum (although the United States largely places the burden of protecting those often-violated rights on individual families) (Ong-Dean 2009; Trainor 2010). Since the passage of these laws, there has been significant research on the implementation and use of computers and assistive technologies in special education programs (Dell, Newton, and Petroff 2011). There is also a growing body of literature on the design and development of interactive technologies as well as robotics for rehabilitative and therapeutic use by children with disabilities (Alper, Hourcade, and Gilutz 2012). Some researchers, influenced by the participatory design movement, have also explored how young people with disabilities can benefit from being directly involved in the development of technology intended for their use, and in turn, how technology is improved by their participation (Guha, Druin, and Fails 2008).

Outside these curricular and experimental contexts, however, scholars have paid little attention to the day-to-day experiences of youth with disabilities when using new media and technology (Bouck, Okolo, and Courtad 2007), including their pleasures and frustrations. To borrow the terminology of Mizuko Ito and her colleagues (2009), youth with disabilities are "hanging out, messing around, [and] geeking out" with digital media too (Alper 2013). This omission reflects the ways in which the recreational activities of individuals with disabilities are primarily seen as an instrumental tool for diagnosis and therapy rather than as something with intrinsic value (Adkins et al. 2013; Goodley and Runswick-Cole 2010). In order to support participation in social, civic, and economic life for *all* young people, we need to know more about the kinds of opportunities that youth with various disabilities regularly have and do not have with information and communication technologies.

The remainder of this introduction serves to unpack the title of this report. The term *digital youth with disabilities* is a loose, fluid category comprised of an incredibly heterogeneous population. It should be noted from the outset that all the research reviewed in this report is subject to children's individual and developmental differences. The insights on disability, children, and parenting presented here are limited to the degree that I do not identify as having a disability, and am not the child of someone with a disability, the parent or sibling of a child with a disability, or a parent at all. The published research discussed and commentary offered is drawn from a number of sources, including an extensive literature review across multiple disciplines, primary research from my dissertation, and participation in workshops and conferences related to individuals with disabilities' media and technology use.[2] In featuring children, adolescents, teenagers, and young adults with disabilities as digital youth, this report rejects the dominant characterizations of individuals with disabilities as deficient and other.

### Defining Youth with Disabilities

As of 2009, youth with disabilities constituted approximately 13 percent of all students ages three to twenty-one, or nearly 6.5 million people (Snyder and Dillow 2012).[3] Students with the following disabilities are eligible for special education and related services under IDEA: autism, deaf-blindness, deafness, developmental delay, emotional disturbance, hearing impairment, intellectual disability, multiple disabilities, orthopedic impairment, other health impairment, specific learning disability, speech or language impairment, traumatic brain injury, or visual impairment (including blindness).[4] The conditions responsible for various impairments may or may not be immediately apparent to others. For example, while the use of crutches or a guide dog may visibly signal a disability, some disabilities (such as autism) are not necessarily easily identifiable through appearance. Some impairments are more permanent (e.g., paralysis), while others are temporary or fluctuate depending on the environment (e.g., chronic fatigue syndrome or multiple chemical sensitivities).

Various government agencies serving children in the United States provide different data about childhood disability. This complicates an understanding of the broader national trends in disability and effective provision of resources. While the numbers supplied by the US Department of Education define a *child with a disability* through the lens of educational performance (and the adverse effects of disability on education), the US Department of Health and Human Services surveys households to identify *children with special health care needs*, defined as "those who have or are at increased risk for a chronic physical, developmental, behavioral, or emotional condition and who also require health and related services of a type or amount beyond that required by children generally" (McPherson et al. 1998, 138). Using this measure, there are an estimated 11.2 million children under the age of eighteen with special health care needs in the United States. Among all households, 23 percent include at least one child with special health care needs (US Department of Health and Human Services 2013).[5]

In addition to these institutional definitions, there are multiple other ways of conceptualizing youth with disabilities. Researchers studying the sociology of childhood contend that the category of youth has evolved over history, and the term *child* is a social construction informed by perceptions of class, race, and disability (James and Prout 1997; Thorne 2009; Safford and Safford 2006). Factors including longer life expectancy, developments in medicine (e.g., vaccination), the introduction of compulsory education, and the enactment of child labor laws have all shaped understandings of children's intrinsic value to society as well as their parents (Zelizer 1994).

In a study of British child care manuals published between 1839 and 1924, Harriet Cooper (2013) traces a gradual shift in the West from concerns about illness and mortality in the nineteenth century to twentieth-century worries about children's abnormality. The idea of the "normal child" has only been in existence since the initial scientific study of child development during that era (Walkerdine 1993; Burman 2008). The normal child is a concept built on classical notions of the ideal body along with the invention of the bell curve, the field of statistics, and associated charts and diagnostic tools (Davis 1995). One "average" child is an amalgam of many—particularly measures of white, Western, male, middle-class children (Burman 2001). Individuals rarely simultaneously exhibit all social, emotional, intellectual, and physical behaviors and characteristics "typical" of that age.

Social constructions of normalcy create the "problem" of the child with a disability, whose chronological or biological age may not match up with their "developmental age." Children with disabilities have historically been subject to gross abuses of power by the able bodied. Many were victims of the eugenics movement in the early twentieth century in efforts to socially engineer "better babies" (Stern 2005). These attempts include institutionalization, sterilization, and physical and sexual abuse (Safford and Safford 2006). There has been no consistent way to define youth with disabilities over the course of US history (Halfon, Houtrow, Larson, and Newacheck 2012). Youth is an evolving concept—one whose history is inherently interdependent with the regulation of children's bodies.

Disability—as a concept, culture, and identity—has changed as well (Nielsen 2012). In the United States, dominant cultural values such as self-reliance, individualism, and "fitting in" shape the ways in which people with disabilities are perceived (Longmore and Umansky 2001). Disability studies scholars contend that a "medical model" underpins prevailing Western views of disability and people with disabilities, meaning that disability is understood as an individualized case of biological burden or deficit. In response to the medical model, some disability activists and scholars emphasize a "social model" of disability, which shifts the focus from the individual to society. The social model makes distinctions between impairment (bodily difference) and disability (the social and built environment that disables as well as discriminates against different bodies) (Oliver 1990; Shakespeare 2013).

Some have critiqued both the medical and social models for overly simplistic notions of disability (Kafer 2013; McRuer 2006; Siebers 2008) as being similar to a false sex/gender binary (Butler 1990). Feminist disability scholars argue for a more fluid definition of "dis/ability" (Sobchack 2004). Rosemarie Garland Thomson (1996, 7) notes that all bodies—depending on the environment, situation, and interaction—have "varying degrees of disability or able-bodiedness, or extra-ordinariness." This fluidity is difficult to express through standardized governmental measures of disability status.

What *is* clear is that each individual with a disability understands their own relationships to disability, their bodies, and society in unique ways (Linton 1998). Language and terminology both reflects and shapes these relationships. The appropriateness of using "identity-first language" (e.g., someone who is deaf) or "person-first language" (e.g., someone with a learning disability) must be understood within the context of specific disabilities and their cultures, which this report aims to respect and value. For example, many within the community of autistic self-advocates (which includes both adults and children) prefer the term *autistic* to *people with autism*. They claim their autism as an inseparable part of their identity—more of a source of pride than an insult (see, for instance, Brown 2011; Fleishmann and Fleishmann 2012). Ultimately, all people should have the right to decide how they would like others to describe them.

### Locating Disability among Digital Youth

Considering the myriad ways in which people with disabilities are often denied agency, it is helpful to draw on research more broadly on underrepresented youth. Many young people in the United States—with an array of racial, ethnic, cultural, and linguistic backgrounds—encounter a "participation gap" (Jenkins et al. 2006) that separates them in nuanced ways from those making the most of online and off-line opportunities and resources. Individuals and groups can leverage information and communication technologies to support greater social engagement, cultural contribution, and political involvement among youth challenging existing power dynamics (Cohen et al. 2012; Watkins 2009). While a complex mix of demographics, use, and expertise shape young people's social and digital exclusion (Livingstone and Helsper 2007), disability tends to be an underrecognized component (Cole et al. 2011; Dobransky and Hargittai

2006). This not only dislocates children and adolescents with disabilities from important discussions of digital youth (Peppler and Warschauer 2012) but also masks the multifaceted ways in which disability and specific disabilities intersect with race, class, ethnicity, nationality, language, and gender in children's lives.

Feminist disability theorist Alison Kafer (2013, 32–33) writes of the figure of the child in US politics that "the always already white Child is also always already healthy and nondisabled; disabled children are not part of this privileged imaginary except as the abject other." Addressing inequality among youth with disabilities necessitates confronting the ways in which class, gender, and race factor into broader conceptions of disability, particularly in the public education and penal systems in the United States (Morris and Morris 2006). For example, while there is no marked disproportion among racial and ethnic groups in low-incidence disability categories (e.g., deaf-blindness), black males are overrepresented in the high-incidence disability categories of intellectual disability, emotional disturbance, and learning disabilities (Aud et al. 2013; Ford 2012). While students with disabilities comprise 13 percent of all US students, they make up 25 percent of students receiving multiple out-of-school suspensions, 23 percent of all students getting a school-related arrest, and 19 percent of expelled students (Lhamon and Samuels 2014). While this report's focus is on home media use, it should be noted that not all youth with disabilities live at home, or do so on a full-time basis. Some are incarcerated, some live in residential facilities, and some spend part of their time in respite facilities.

"Digital divide" rhetoric tends to naturalize underrepresented youth as outsiders to technological progress and masks structural inequalities (Everett 2008a). The irony is that the technological world as we know it has actually been fundamentally shaped by youth with disabilities who found their way around complex systems. In the 1950s, for instance, blind youth were among the first to discover that they could "hack" the telephone system using perfect pitch to trigger automated switches—a phenomenon known as "phone phreaking" (Rosenbaum 1971). They became central figures in the history of hacking, and have been directly cited by Apple founders Steve Jobs and Steve Wozniak as highly influential (Lapsley 2013).

Youth with disabilities in the United States tend to be made visible for the political purposes of others. When culturally depicted as "poster children," they are defined exclusively by their medical needs (Longmore 2013). Each child with a disability also has abilities, hobbies, and personal preferences. Considering the slogan of the disability rights movement, "Nothing about Us without Us" (Charlton 2000), there is a pressing need to invite youth with disabilities and the important people in their lives into the dialogue about new media and participatory culture, where they have much to contribute when it comes to reshaping and bettering society.

### The Role of Families

The promises and pitfalls of children's media use, and specifically among those with disabilities, are also bundled up with policies impacting families, such as affordable health care and access to health insurance, the living wage, and the increasing costs of child care in the United States. For example, Sue Lin, Stella Yu, and Robin Harwood (2012) found that autistic children and those with other developmental disabilities from immigrant families are more than twice as likely as nonimmigrant families to lack consistent care, and three times as likely to lack any type of US health care coverage. Family income below the federal poverty level is also associated with a higher prevalence of parent-reported developmental disabilities (Boyle et al. 2011). Families of children with disabilities reflect this country's racial, ethnic, socioeconomic, cultural, and linguistic diversity, and may have little else in common with one another.

Caring for youth with disabilities in the United States also has a number of gendered dimensions, as highlighted by various feminist disability studies scholars (Adams 2013; Jack 2014; Landsman 2009). In earlier generations, US children with disabilities and complex medical issues were more likely to be institutionalized than live at home with their parents and in their communities (Metzel and Walker 2001). In the mid-twentieth century, the "refrigerator mother theory," popularized by psychologist Bruno Bettelheim, naturalized the placing of blame for children's autism on their supposedly "cold" and emotionally distant mothers. This era was also marked by the relocation of many young families from the cities to the suburbs, displacing mothers from their existing networks of friends and family who might have otherwise assisted with child care. Some argue that the United States is currently in the midst of a cultural shift away from the refrigerator mother archetype toward a neoliberal "intensive mothering" paradigm (Hays 1996). Instead of being recipients of misplaced blame, today's ideal "warrior-hero mothers are now responsible for curing the disability, or at least accessing the intervention that will mitigate the disability's impact on their children" (Sousa 2011, 221).

The scenarios of the refrigerator mother and warrior-hero mother both define disability as something to be eradicated, or that should be prevented. Difficulties in obtaining health insurance and government support as well as a lack of reliable, culturally appropriate, and community-based resources often result in family members (mostly mothers) foregoing employment to fill caretaking roles in households with people with disabilities (Scott 2010). Though families of children with disabilities frequently experience concrete difficulties such as financial hardship, they are unfairly stigmatized and viewed through a lens of tragedy in US society, as if in a state of perpetual crisis and in need of charity (Green 2003). For many families, disability can be a source of pride as well as a positive aspect of their and their child's identity (Rapp and Ginsburg 2011). Many parents of children with disabilities, working alongside adults with disabilities, have been important advocates and members of the US disability rights movement (Shapiro 1993).[6]

Starting in the 1960s, human development and family relations researchers began to question these preconceived assumptions about families of children with disabilities and test them empirically (Barsch 1961). Resiliency theory (Patterson 2002) suggests that families of children with disabilities develop accommodations, or "proactive efforts of a family to adapt, exploit, counterbalance, and react to the many competing and sometimes contradictory forces in their lives" (Bernheimer, Gallimore, and Weisner 1990, 223). Rather than equating disability with adversity, "a child ought not to be routinely described as a stressor or a nonnormative demand on families who may perceive them otherwise" (Maul and Singer 2009, 157). Families of children with disabilities face significant challenges but also have unique strengths (Solomon 2012).

Media can play a significant role in family accommodations. A number of researchers have found that families often alter their technology and media use in order to adapt to their child with a disability, and make family life more harmonious (see, for example, Maul and Singer 2009; Shane and Albert 2008; Nally, Houton, and Ralph 2000). Some accommodate for behavior difficulties by providing DVD players when their children ride in the car. Others take proactive efforts to make changes in their television-viewing habits at home, including having separate screens for different family members, watching child-oriented programming together, reducing background television, or not watching any television at all (Keilty and Galvin 2006). Parents might use media as a reward for painful treatments or long hospital stays (Mattingly 2003).

Accordingly, this report does not presume that children with disabilities are a stressor on family life or family media use. Research on parenting decisions about children's media use indicates that these choices are not made independent of other caregiving behaviors (see, for example, Clark 2013; Katz 2014; Seiter 1999). Parents and other primary caregivers of young people with disabilities (i.e., foster parents or grandparents) make decisions about media consistent with their beliefs about successful family functioning—beliefs that are in part shaped by their racial, ethnic, cultural, and class backgrounds.

## Summary

Insights from the fields of feminist disability studies, the sociology of childhood, and human development and family relations are helpful for understanding the broader issues shaping what it means to raise digital youth with disabilities in the United States today. Supporting the societal participation of young people with disabilities calls for critical and purposeful inquiry into the overlapping intersections of youth and disability, disability and digital media, and disability and child rearing. The relationships between these various elements are always evolving, bound up with broader historical, social, cultural, economic, and political shifts in the United States that impact how families thrive.

While this report is written primarily for fellow researchers and scholars, my aim is that it is accessible and comprehendible for a general audience beyond academia, technology, and policy circles. Parents of children with disabilities often feel uncertain about the appropriateness of media and technology in their children's lives (Durkin and Conti-Ramsden 2014). The professionals who work in educational and therapeutic contexts with youth with disabilities rarely have a background in children's media use, are frequently ignorant about new media, and are in need of professional development in the classroom to support their own understanding of digital media and integrating technology into curriculum. Parents also express feeling that professionals lack an understanding of their own family media habits (Nally, Houlton, and Ralph 2000).

The following chapters place disability in the center of our understanding of children's recreational experiences and informal learning with new media. Chapter 2 focuses on the notion of *screen time*, a phrase coined by the American Academy of Pediatrics (AAP) and readily adopted by the mainstream press that refers to children's time spent with screen-based media. Screen time is generally employed in a pejorative manner—for example, through public service campaigns aimed at parents to reduce children's screen time. While other scholars have pointed out how this terminology is particularly problematic, new angles to these arguments emerge when considering children with disabilities along with their and their families' varied use of media (e.g., students who use augmentative and assistive communication devices in the form of iPads as their primary mode of communication, or autistic children who use media to make connections to others).

Chapter 3 delves deeper into how young people with various disabilities use media to socialize with their caregivers, siblings, and friends. Youth with disabilities are frequently stereotyped as being socially isolated, and new media have historically been imagined as both being the cause and cure for this segregation. The existing research, however, suggests a much more complex story than the one presented by these technologically and socially determinist discourses. Chapter 4 explores issues that parents of youth with certain disabilities (e.g., attention deficit hyperactivity disorder [ADHD] or autism) specifically encounter in selecting, managing, and purchasing media for their child. Beyond considering children's individual preferences and needs, this chapter also raises critical awareness of external factors shaping the media and technology available to youth with disabilities—namely, the limits of existing platforms, content, and age standards. In chapter 5, I conclude with a discussion of future research directions.

## 2 The Trouble with Screen Time

How young people spend their unsupervised time outside school has concerned adults ever since formal education became compulsory in the United States in the late nineteenth and early twentieth centuries (Wartella and Robb 2008). While today's children, adolescents, and teenagers continue to spend part of their spare waking hours with older media forms such as terrestrial radio and print books, screen-based and social media play a prominent role in most young people's daily lives. Children under age eight spend an average of one hour and fifty-five minutes using screen media daily (including television, DVDs, computers, video games, and mobile devices) (Rideout 2013). Three out of four US teenagers visit social media sites (e.g., Facebook or Twitter) at least once a day (Madden et al. 2013), and one in four use at least two types of social media daily (Rideout 2012). Much of this increased social media use is attributed to the sharp rise in smartphone adoption among US teens, up from 23 percent in 2011 to 37 percent in 2013 (Madden et al. 2013).

For many parents, screen time is a phrase they commonly hear in mainstream press reports on kids and media—for example, "Too Much Screen Time Can Threaten Attention Span" (Doheny 2010) and "Screen Time Higher than Ever for Children" (Lewin

2011). The term emerged in the 2000s, and refers (usually negatively) to children's overall time spent with media through any
screen-based information and communication technology.[1] The
AAP (2001, 1224) advises pediatricians to talk to parents about
children's media use and discuss "limiting screen time (including television, videos, computer and video games) to 1 to 2 hours
per day" for all children.[2] A more recent AAP (2013, 959) position statement backpedals a bit, specifying that the guidelines
only pertain to children's time spent with "entertainment screen
media." These limits, the academy explains, are due to research
that points to children's excessive screen time being strongly
related to a myriad of negative health effects, including obesity
(AAP 2011) and substance abuse (AAP 2010). Furthermore, the
AAP (n.d.) discourages any screen media use for children under
age two, stating, "Young children learn best by interacting with
people, not screens."

The picture painted by the AAP is not entirely dark. To be
fair, the newest AAP (2013) statement lends some credence to
the potential benefits of educational media for children. Yet the
generic, pejorative usage of screen time remains culturally per-
vasive (Sarachan 2012). Apps geared toward parents with titles
such as *Screen Time: Parental Control* and *Screen Time—Media Time
Manager* have capitalized on the term. Since 2011, the Campaign
for a Commercial Free Childhood (CCFC 2013) has organized
Screen-Free Week, a seven-day period during which families are
encouraged to "turn off screens and turn on life."[3]

Equating the reduction of screen time with an increase in
families' "quality time" reflects the longing for an idealized
notion of family life that has never existed for most Americans
at any single point in US history (Coontz 1992). Such ideals are
based on the dominant image of the nuclear family—one that is

white, English speaking, and middle class, with two heterosexual biological parents and able-bodied family members. While few would take issue with the AAP and CCFC's basic concern for children's health and well-being, the ways in which screen time is defined and targeted as a problem merits careful consideration.

In this chapter, following some historical background on the idea of screen time and a summary of its main critiques, I discuss how the concept is particularly problematic with respect to youth with disabilities and their families. I argue that the medical discourse around children's screen time produces a particular bodily standard that is projected as the ideal child. This rhetoric frames disability as a diminished state of childhood. Sweeping generalizations about screen time for children of all ages obscure the multifaceted nature of screen media use by youth with disabilities. Families should be able to interact with one another socially with or without screens, as necessary.

### Screen Time: A Brief History

The term screen time and its circulation through the US mainstream press must be put in context with the expert advice that parents have historically received about managing young people's screen media use, starting with television (Jenkins 1998). Postwar baby boom families were among the earliest adopters of television and first market for television advertisers (Spigel 1992). Over the 1950s, Americans installed television sets into their homes at a more rapid pace than any information and communication technology to come before or after (DeGusta 2012). During this era, developmental psychologists (more so than pediatricians) offered advice about television's impact on children (Rich 2007). Mothers with growing child care responsibilities

readily found advice about managing children's television viewing in newspapers and popular magazines. These messages were
mixed. Some child development experts expressed concerns
about television's physical, psychological, and cognitive effects;
others were hopeful about television as a site of family together-
ness and learning; and some found the impact of television to be
negligible (Seiter 1995).

Even in television's first decade, a specific focus on children's
excessive time spent watching television appears in the popular press (Wartella and Reeves 1985; Wartella and Robb 2008).
For example, a *New York Times* article titled "Youngsters 5 to 6
Give 4 Hours to TV" (1950) concludes that the more time children devote to television, the less time they dedicate to reading,
studying, and engaging in creative and outdoor play. A 1957 *Los
Angeles Times* article suggests that such press stories concentrating on the quantity of children's television viewing were par for
the course during the decade. The author notes, "Every so often
a report is published about the number of hours a day children
spend watching television," and that taken together, they con-
vey "a frightening statistic" (Downer 1957). Statistical fragments
on rates of screen media use, strung together without context,
have historically influenced parental beliefs about the negative
impact of media, which Ellen Seiter (1999, 6) refers to as "'lay
theories' of media effects."

Contemporary calls to reduce screen time are rooted in the
"television-free" movement that first emerged in the 1970s.
Advocacy from the medical field about the negative effects
of media on children also arose during this era, whereas prior
research was predominantly based in the fields of psychology and communication (Rich 2007). Reporting on the 1971
National Symposium on Children and Television, sponsored by

the parent group Action for Children's Television, the *Hartford Courant* led with the headline "Screen Time Calculated" (1975). The article largely consisted of statistics describing "the sheer volume of television youngsters watch." According to Nielsen ratings, by 1980, half of US households reported owning multiple television sets, and the market for video game consoles, personal computers, and portable music players grew over the course of the decade as well. The changing television landscape during the 1980s included a proliferation of cable and more hours of programming geared toward children than ever before (Hendershot 1998, 2004; Turow 1981).

In 1988, the AAP released its first television policy statement, titled "Commercialization of Children's Television and Its Effect on Imaginative Play." The statement included the recommendations that parents be warned about the dangers of "prolonged television viewing" and "limit the amount of time their children spend watching television" (AAP 1988, 900). The AAP's (1990) statement on "Children, Adolescents, and Television" added the recommendation that pediatricians advise parents to limit their children's television time to one to two hours per day. The academy also sought legislative support for the Children's Television Act of 1990, which required licensed broadcasters to air at least three hours of educational children's programming per week.

At the turn of the century, screens in US and other Western homes diversified and become more plentiful. Parents expressed growing concern about a shift from proximally shared living room experiences to children's physically isolated but digitally networked media use in bedrooms (Bovill and Livingstone 2001). A 1997 article in the *New York Times* on a Pulling the Plug week at an elementary school in the suburbs of New York City illustrates the other screen-based media drawn into campaigns such as Television-Free Week, launched in 1994. "My concern is screen time," notes the vice president of the school district's board of education. "Parents make a distinction about videos and computer games, but that still reduces the amount of time left for play that a child has" (Rosenberg 1997). While the amount and types of screen media in US homes today are different from the 1950s, the present-day preoccupation with framing the relationship between children and media through the metric of time is an echo of the past.

## Arguments against Screen Time

A number of scholars, journalists, and cultural critics have questioned the usefulness of screen time as a concept (see, for example, Guernsey 2014; Kleeman 2010, 2012), and argued for more nuanced conversations about children's experiences with media (Buckingham 2006). The main criticisms marshaled against screen time are as follows: screen time is determinist, it makes overgeneralizations about media content, it oversimplifies how families understand time, it does not displace nonscreen-based activities, and it does not distinguish between different types of screens. These critiques are explained below, along with dimensions of these contentions that speak specifically to the experiences of families of children with disabilities.

### Screen Time Is Technologically and Socially Determinist

Screen time is a technologically determinist concept in that it categorizes screen media as an inherently bad influence on children. On the flip side, it is also socially determinist—a form of moral panic (Cohen 1972) about the fear of literally and figuratively leaving kids to their own devices. Screen time presents children (especially girls) as intrinsically vulnerable to technology (Cassell and Cramer 2008). It is not that technology alone is empowering or disempowering to children, however, or that children will inherently use technology in either positive or negative ways. Rather, children's relationship with new media is more interdependent (Buckingham 2006). Social class and cultural background informs families' perceptions about the "proper" use and value of media in the home (Clark 2013; Hoover, Clark, and Alters 2004).

The determinist rhetoric of screen time extends beyond concerns with children's well-being. Antitelevision metaphors (e.g., the "plug-in drug"; Marie Winn 1985, 1987) have tremendous rhetorical sway in the US and Europe (Buckingham 1993). Television, as a medium, is constructed through these metaphors as a scapegoat for late twentieth-century social issues and cultural anxieties about drug abuse, gun violence, and teen pregnancy (Mittell 2000). This language strongly associates "improper" media use with poor and working-class, nonwhite children (ibid.; Seiter 2005, 2007). Calls for screen time limits are a diversion from larger institutional factors that impact children and their families (Seiter 1999).

Determinist discourse around children and screen media use is particularly pronounced when it comes to youth with disabilities. Parents frequently encounter mixed messages in the press about the relationship between children, disability, and media. These messages tend to depict youth with disabilities as defenseless and in need of protection, or as symbols of overcoming adversity and inspiration for people without disabilities (Haller 2010). Headlines about the media and technology use of children with disabilities vacillate between alarmist rhetoric, such as "Boys with Autism or ADHD More Prone to Overuse Video

Games" (Shute 2013), and techno-utopian language, like "iPad Opens World to a Disabled Boy" (Hager 2010). Such stories tend to obscure the complex sociocultural, political, and economic factors that play a part in children's encounters with technology, for better and worse, in their everyday lives. These reports in the mainstream media also generally fail to include the perspectives of individuals with disabilities communicating on their own behalf about their media use and technology habits (see, for instance, Clarke 2012).

### Screen Time Makes Overgeneralizations about Screen-Based Content

The AAP specifically targets entertainment screen media in its suggestions about screen time limits. In doing so, it pathologizes the pleasures that children and their families may derive from such content. For example, the National Institutes of Health contends carte blanche that "computers can be helpful when kids are using them to do schoolwork. But surfing the Internet, spending time on Facebook, or watching YouTube videos is considered unhealthy screen time" (Kaneshiro 2011). This statement does not consider the range of material on Web sites, usefulness of this material to children in their daily lives, or ways in which individuals and groups of children interpret media texts.

The AAP's position on children's leisure is deeply historically rooted in critiques of mass-produced culture (Benjamin 1968) and a condescending attitude toward "the masses" for being duped by the culture industry (Adorno and Horkheimer 2002). Painting consumers as unwitting victims underestimates the agency of audiences along with the ways in which people creatively interpret and remake mass media into something that better fits their own lives (Appadurai 1996; Ginsburg,

Abu-Lughod, and Larkin 2002; Radway 1984). Media texts provide a shared set of meanings and experiences for young people and their social partners to draw from in constructing as well as maintaining a sense of reality (Dyson 2003; Jenkins 2006; Pugh 2009). Popular media provide contexts for families to stay connected through activities such as playing, reading, and creating media (Lull 1990; Morley 1988; Clark 2013).

Another angle on the critique that screen time essentializes mass culture is that it overlooks the ways in which media use, outside purely "educational" content, can be particularly meaningful for different groups of youth with disabilities who may be socially excluded in other areas of their lives (see, for example, Belcher and Herr-Stephenson 2011; King-Sears, Swanson, and Mainzer 2011; Moni and Jobling 2008). Popular video games, as a cultural touchstone, can be a conduit for social acceptance for youth with disabilities (Pitaru 2008). In her ethnographic study of black children with significant disabilities and chronic illnesses, anthropologist Cheryl Mattingly (2003, 2006) found that children and their caregivers formed an "interpretive community" around children's mass media. They took up Disney characters and plots, reimagining and remaking them to resist the stigmatized identities that surround disability, race, and class. Media that is "good" for children is not always curriculum heavy. By lumping entertainment screen media into a totalizing negative category, the AAP does not reflect the nuanced ways that popular culture can be meaningful to youth, especially young people with disabilities.

### Screen Time Oversimplifies How Families Understand Time

Sociologists have illustrated (often through qualitative research methods) that not all families think of time in the same ways

(Lareau 2000; Nippert-Eng 1996). Parents have different beliefs about the management and value of time, also known as a family's "temporal orientation" (Jordan 1992). While the AAP's screen time limits emphasize quantity (e.g., hours spent playing video games), families experience the passage of time in other ways, such as through patterns, routines, and rituals (Hochschild 1989, 1997). The meaning of screen time within a given family cannot be understood apart from a household's temporal ideologies.

Time may also take on different meanings among children with disabilities and their families. Families tend to adjust the timing of their daily lives to accommodate the needs of their child with a disability (Maul and Singer 2009). For example, travel time can take longer when a person with a physical disability encounters a mode of transportation that is difficult to access. Conversations may happen at a different rate with someone who uses an augmentative and alternative communication device. "Family mealtime" may happen more or less frequently depending on any feeding issues that a child with cerebral palsy might have. Screen media can sometimes help routines run more smoothly in households. Some autistic children, for instance, find low-cost visual schedule software and apps for mobile devices helpful for self-regulation (Hayes et al. 2010).

Various disability scholars discuss the notion of "crip time" as a more flexible alternative to normative time frames (Gill 1995; Zola 1993). Disability can shape people's relationships with time, for individuals with disabilities and anyone who spends time with them. Crip time provokes the examination of norms and expectations about the pace, scheduling, and duration of human activities (Kafer 2013), including that of household routines. Screen time is based on particular normative expectations about how children's bodies relate to time, screens, and other people's bodies.

## Screen Time Does Not Displace Nonscreen-Based Activities

A primary argument used to promote screen time limits is the time-displacement theory (Hornik 1981; Maccoby 1951). The main idea behind the displacement hypothesis is that children spend less time doing traditionally nondigitally mediated activities than they used to (e.g., going outside, learning musical instruments, participating in imaginative play, reading print books, or doing homework), and that the primary cause for this decrease is that children are replacing their engagement in these activities with screen media use.

There is no longitudinal empirical evidence, however, in support of the displacement theory (Mutz, Roberts, and van Vuuren 1993). The theory presumes that nondigitally mediated forms of activities such as reading and exercise will automatically replace screen media once they are turned off. Yet it is difficult to determine if the presence or absence of media in the home causes an increase or decrease in certain nonscreen-based activities without also examining individual families' general belief structures, values, and norms (Krcmar 2009).

The displacement hypothesis is also unsupported with regard to youth with disabilities. A number of studies have found that children, adolescents, and teenagers with disabilities tend to spend more time with screen-based media at home than youth without disabilities (Lidström, Ahlsten, and Hemmingsson 2011; Lo 2013; Mazurek et al. 2012). It isn't clear whether that time would otherwise be spent engaged in physical activity, though. It might be that increased media use is in fact related to the high cost of adapted sports equipment, lack of inclusive physical education programs at school, and few affordable community-based recreational programs, accessible playgrounds for children, and sensory-friendly play spaces. While imaginative play is held up as a "better" use of children's time than screen time, not all children have the same capacity or interest in free play (Goodley and Runswick-Cole 2010). While campaigns such as Screen-Free Week equate the reduction of media use with an increase in children's well-being, such claims are not grounded in causal evidence that rule out all the other possible factors that influence children's activities and family functioning.

### Screen Time Does Not Recognize the Affordances and Constraints of Different Screens

Screen time recommendations generally tend to deem some screens "good" (e.g., computers) and others "bad" (e.g., televisions). This inherently privileges economically advantaged children because the better screens are cost prohibitive, as is the infrastructure that supports their optimal use (e.g., broadband Internet) (Seiter 2005, 2007). The computers that aid in the creation of schoolwork (i.e., those that have keyboards and advanced software) are much more expensive than computers that lack such functionality (i.e., smartphones). Some screens make it far easier for a child to consume media content than create or circulate it. Different platforms and digital devices that families own have a range of design affordances as well as constraints that shape use.

At the same time, campaigns such as those run by the CCFC that encourage families to temporarily go "screen free" and "unplug" treat all screens as a blight on households. Unplugging associates turning off all screen media devices with physical renewal and spiritual serenity (hence, it is sometimes referred to as a "digital detox" or "Digital Sabbath"). The idea that temporarily letting go of electronic media recharges a family's bond has existed at least since the introduction of television into homes (see, for example, Bradbury 1950). But being able to take a digital "vacation," with a clear start and end date, is a kind of privilege. People with more power and agency have a broader range of choices about what they do (and don't do) with technology.

In this manner, campaigns encouraging families to unplug enforce a form of ableist privilege over children with disabilities and their families. Unplugging assumes that declaring human independence from screen media is beneficial, clear-cut, and easy to implement as long as a family is personally committed. Yet different bodies have different kinds of relationships with communication technologies, beyond a simple binary of dependence and independence (Balsamo 1995). Smartphones and tablet computers—as media creation, consumption, and circulation tools—can be a primary or vital form of communication for children who have difficulty or prefer not to use embodied oral speech. For example, texting can be a key form of communication and self-expression for deaf youth (Bakken 2005). Going screen free cannot be reduced to a simple personal or family choice.

## Ableism and the Medicalization of Screen Time

In addition to these critiques of the AAP's broad guidelines around screen time and the platform they provide for antimedia advocacy groups, the remainder of this chapter highlights a largely neglected flaw underpinning screen time edicts. Screen time is an inherently political issue in that only certain groups have the power and agency to shape the public conversation

about children and media. Arguments that new media technologies stunt social, emotional, and neurological development (see,
for instance, Turkle 2011; Carr 2010) pervade the popular press,
instilling mild anxiety and doubt in parents, particularly caregivers of young children (Guernsey 2012).

The cultural power of screen time is largely derived from its
association with medical discourse, which naturalizes children's
media use as a public health issue. Medical opinions about media
in children's lives are granted more authority in US society than
other groups with expertise concerning young people, such as
the fields of child care and education (Rogow 2013; Seiter 1999).
The latter positions are more often associated with female and
lower-class labor, and are given less authority than the traditionally male-dominated medical fields. A full analysis of the moral
panic around screen time through the lens of feminist theory is
beyond the scope of this report, but for now, it is important to
highlight the way in which the public regulation of children's
media behaviors is intertwined with patriarchy.

A further danger lies in primarily associating children's
complex relationships with media and technology with the
terminology of medical science. According to scholars of the
sociology of medicine, definitions and treatments of health and
illness are part of a wider system of social control by the medical professions as well as the state (Foucault 1973). New media
technologies are frequently based on particular assumptions
about subjectivity and agency (Star 1991), and are designed
with certain assumptions about individual competency in mind
(Moser 2006). I contend that the medical language that underpins screen time is based on normative conceptions of the ideal
child and particular standards of children's bodies—specifically
their *nutrition* and *physical activity*, how they *sleep*, and how they
focus their *attention*.[4]

## Nutrition, Physical Activity, and Obesity

Forms of mass culture (e.g., cartoons and popular literature) have historically been linked to metaphors of "junk food" and eating (Spigel 1992). The characterization of children's time spent with television as an unhealthy consumption habit began to appear in the 1950s—an era that also saw a sharp rise in the production of consumer goods marketed to children, such as cereal and bubblegum (Seiter 1995). For example, in a 1952 *Chicago Tribune* article with the headline "Control Time Child Spends at the Television Set," parents are urged to manage children's "intake" of television programs in the same way that they set limits on sweets (Marcia Winn 1952). Adult anxieties about children's pleasures are reflected in descriptions of the iPhone as habit forming and "sticky" like candy in the hands of young children (Cannon and Barker 2012). In *Everything Bad Is Good for You*, author Stephen Johnson (2005, 211) popularized the notion that children should consume a "balanced diet" of media including some of the bad with the good stuff.

The media-as-consumption metaphor is problematic for a number of reasons. First, it reduces the complex relationship that people have with popular media to a one-way relationship (Radway 1986). It becomes difficult to characterize children as anything but passive in their relationship with mass culture. Second, the discourse of the media diet runs into an issue at the heart of debates over how to reduce childhood obesity in the United States and serious, related individual health issues, including high blood pressure and insulin resistance. The degree to which people choose the media they spend time with as well as the food they eat and physical activities they partake in is subject to genetic influences, stress and related issues, and environmental factors beyond just the scope of the individual. Lastly, and most significant, the data do not support the hypothesis that simply unplugging media will reduce childhood obesity. Findings suggest that while there is some relationship between screen media use and obesity (for example, through the advertising of nonnutritious foods), it is unclear how, and for which children, media is and is not implicated in increased caloric intake along with decreased activity level (Vandewater and Cummings 2011).

Obesity and secondary issues become even more complex when disability is taken into account as a risk factor. According to the National Health and Nutrition Examination Survey, 22.5 percent of US children with disabilities are obese compared to 16 percent of children without disabilities. While children with disabilities are at a higher risk of childhood obesity than typically developing children (particularly girls and young teenagers), this varies by disability (Rimmer, Rowland, and Yamaki 2007). Better data are needed to determine appropriate measures for health and fitness for individuals. For instance, the body mass index has been shown to have limited applicability to children with paralysis (Liususan, Abresch, and McDonald 2004). Children with disabilities also often have a more complex relationship with food than children without disabilities. Medications can increase food cravings, and specific disabilities may come with food issues and aversions.

The research on media and obesity that the AAP cites has focused almost exclusively on youth without disabilities. The health behaviors of children with disabilities are complicated by a number of family stressors. As Paula Minihan, Sarah Fitch, and Aviva Must (2007, 69) write, "Time and money needed to arrange for healthy meals, increasing physical activity and reducing screen time may be harder for families [of children with disabilities] also struggling with finances, caretaker time and energy, and pressures associated with employment." Instead of displacing exercise, increased time spent with media among youth with disabilities may instead compensate for time not spent engaged in outdoor physical activity for various reasons (e.g., a child who tires easily or has sensory needs such as being photosensitive). It is unclear if there is a causal or correlational relationship between screen time and obesity among youth with disabilities.

The AAP policy statement does not recognize that sedentary behaviors, in the context of families, shape and are shaped by disability. The National Institutes of Health pathologizes screen time as a "sedentary activity, or being inactive while sitting down. Very little energy is used during screen time" (Kaneshiro 2011). Some youth with disabilities actually expend a good deal of energy in order to use technology. Computer eye gaze systems and switch controls required for some children to engage with media can put strenuous demands on mental concentration as well as physical exertion. One child's sedentary media use can be another child's conservation of precious energy. The child who, for any number of reasons, spends much of their time "inactive while sitting down" (e.g., in a wheelchair) is rendered deviant in their screen time because their bodies do not conform to dominant societal conceptions of health and wellness.

### Sleep

Poor sleep can negatively impact children in a number of ways, including effects on eating habits, behavior, mood, and learning. Medical and public health research has concentrated in recent decades on the relationship between children's screen media use and sleep. Studies have found that children who spend more time with screen media also tend to have a more difficult time falling asleep and are more resistant to going to bed (Garrison, Liekweg, and Christakis 2011; Owens et al. 1999). The stimulation of media, researchers contend, disrupts a child's ability to self-regulate and wind down (Thompson and Christakis 2005). A number of studies have specifically looked at the relationship between sleep and screen media use among children with disabilities. Christopher Engelhardt, Micah Mazurek, and Kristin Sohl (in press) found that access to television or a computer in the bedroom was associated with less sleep among autistic boys ages eight to seventeen, but not so among boys with ADHD of the same age.

Discovering a "link" between sleep and screen media use (what is known as a "correlation" in statistical terms) is not the same as identifying a causal relationship. There may be other factors that cause both screen media use to increase and sleep to decrease among youth with disabilities. Irregular sleep schedules may be due to seizures, anxiety, gastrointestinal problems, or certain medications. Screen media use may be less of a direct cause of sleep deprivation in children with disabilities and more of a symptom of not being able to fall back to sleep for various reasons. The AAP's screen time recommendations presuppose a particular normality to children's sleeping habits and patterns. An "average" night of sleep between two children can look quite different depending on a range of sensory, hormonal, and neurological factors.

### Attention and Hyperactivity

The mainstream press also frequently warns parents that decreased attention span and increased hyperactivity are "side effects" of screen time. Television has in particular historically been positioned as a "drug," having both sedative and overstimulating effects on children (Marie Winn 1985, 1987). Children are figured in this discourse as the population most vulnerable to the narcotizing effects of mass culture (Newman 2010). Media effects researchers have argued that screen media, especially video games, exacerbate attention problems and learning difficulties in children and adolescents (Christakis et al. 2004; Gentile et al. 2012; Swing et al. 2010; Zimmerman and Christakis 2007).

Yet there is no conclusive evidence that screen media negatively impairs children's psychosocial adjustment. In a sample of over eleven thousand children through the UK Millennium Cohort study, Alison Parkes and her colleagues (2013) discovered no relationship between the amount of watching television and playing electronic games at five years old, and attention and hyperactivity at seven years old. Since most of the North American research on ADHD and screen media is not longitudinal in nature, it is a poor indicator of change in children's development over time.

Among children who have already been diagnosed with ADHD, though, there has been little actual research conducted on the role that media plays in their lives. Frustratingly, findings of research conducted on children *without* ADHD are often used to draw conclusions about children who do have the disorder (Christakis et al. 2004). Such claims can be highly misleading. For example, some research has indicated that children with ADHD are actually *less* prone than elementary-school-age children without ADHD to have their cognitive processing negatively impacted by television viewing (Acevedo-Polakovich et al. 2006). The research that does exist on the relationship between media use and children with ADHD has usually been limited to a small sample size, and is based on parent reports (see, for example, Milich and Lorch 1994). It would be negligent to suggest with a high degree of confidence that there is a causal relationship between television viewing and ADHD without additional research proof.

Some parents of children with ADHD find that watching television is an activity they especially enjoy doing with their child because their child can sit relatively quietly for extended periods of time (Milich, Lorch, and Berthiaume 2005). In a survey of attitudes toward television among seventy-seven parents of elementary-school-age children with ADHD, the statement "Television makes children hyperactive" elicited the lowest level of agreement out of fourteen items (other statements included "Television takes up too much of a child's time" and "Television teaches bad habits") (Acevedo-Polakovich, Lorch, and Milich 2007). While the screen time discourse reinforces negative associations between attention and media, use and attitudes toward media among caregivers of children with ADHD may differ significantly from that of families of young people without the disorder.

## Summary

While screen time makes for a rather sensational news headline, it is one that may be losing its relevance. A recent survey suggests that only 30 percent of US parents of children under age eight are "very" or "somewhat" concerned about their children's screen time, and are more concerned about their health and safety, fitness and nutrition, and social-emotional skills (Wartella et al. 2013). We should be suspect of the assumption that screen time is a helpful tool in the first place. The findings of Parkes and colleagues' (2013, 347) longitudinal research in the United Kingdom "do not demonstrate that interventions to reduce screen exposure will improve psychosocial adjustment. Indeed, they suggest that interventions in respect of family and child characteristics, rather than a narrow focus on screen exposure, are more likely to improve outcomes."

The pronouncements of child development experts can exacerbate parental (and particularly maternal) guilt, especially for those encountering challenging life experiences (Seiter 1999). Lynn Clark (2013) critiques uniform media guidelines for assuming that parenting is rational and logical. Instead, emotion work (Hochschild 1983) done by parents plays a significant role in how they manage the risks and benefits of media in their families' lives. The AAP policy position wrongly assumes that digital media impacts US families of all socioeconomic, racial, ethnic, linguistic, and disability backgrounds in the same manner.

Screen time guidelines are grounded in a US-centered belief that parents are the strongest influence on their children's engagement with media. That focus distracts from potential conversations about distributed policy issues that greatly impact children's experiences with technology (Buckingham 2006; Buckingham and Sefton-Green 1997). In the United States, these include uneven broadband Internet access, media consolidation and government deregulation around net neutrality, and a lack of gender and racial diversity in ownership within the entertainment and telecommunications industries. Such issues are not solved by calls to action for stricter ratings systems, content-blocking software, and other strategies to prevent the negative impact of media on children. There are many factors that shape families' lives that have nothing to do with their individual choices.

In addition to existing critiques of screen time, the AAP's edicts are flawed because they are designed around the social scientific standardization of children's bodies first developed in the late nineteenth and early twentieth centuries. They presume a child whose relationship with food and exercise, sleeping patterns, and attention span would be "normal" were it not for the deleterious effects of media use. Discussions about the best uses of media and technology in children's lives need to also consider the functions of different kinds of screen media, what children are expressing about themselves through their engagement with these technologies, and how adults interpret and respond to children's digital media use in particular social contexts (see chapter 3).

# 3 Youth Sociality through and around Media

As early as the introduction of the phonograph, relatively new media technologies have been imagined as both isolating children and drawing them closer to family members and peers (Flichy 2006; Marvin 1998; Spigel 1992). What has changed is that young people's engagement with information and communication technologies occurs in increasingly complex, interconnected social contexts (boyd 2014). They use communication technologies to interact with others who may or may not be physically colocated. For example, a child might use their computer to Skype with a friend in another country—while sending a text to a parent just outside shouting range.

In addition to being social *through* media platforms, children also socialize with copresent others *around* many kinds of media (Silverstone and Hirsch 1992). Families listen to CDs together in the car, teenagers go to movie theaters with their friends, and siblings play with their own video game consoles on separate ends of the living room sofa. Households in developed countries own more media and more types of media than ever before, enabling greater individual and personalized use among family members (Bovill and Livingstone 2001). What it means for young people to be social with media is a constantly shifting target.

Historically, media technologies (from radios to computers) have been understood as both causes of social isolation among youth with disabilities and a means of connection and belonging (see, for instance, Kirkpatrick 2012). This chapter surveys the literature on the sociality of youth with various disabilities around and through old as well as new media, and highlights areas for further study. I specifically examine the ways in which parents, siblings, peers, and individuals outside a child's local community serve as social partners. To begin, the following section provides an overview of theoretical approaches for understanding the sociality and social context of young people's media use.

## Theoretical Approaches

Empirical studies on the role of media in children's development often "control" for complex variables like social norms, peer influences, and cultural practices, rather than addressing what children's lives really look like outside a laboratory setting (Jordan 2004). Increasingly, children and media scholars (see, for example, Takeuchi and Levine, 2014; Vandewater 2013) have argued that such work would be improved by drawing on what is known as the "ecological systems model" of human development, a prominent theory in the field of developmental psychology.[1] First proposed by Urie Bronfenbrenner (1979, 1986, 2005), the ecological systems model highlights the myriad ways in which social systems directly and indirectly influence children's development beyond the immediate context of the parent-child relationship.

The ecological systems model of child development proposes that children are involved in a variety of interconnected social settings and institutions that have direct or indirect impacts on their lives. Bronfenbrenner positioned children at the center of multiple interrelated or "nested" systems (certainly a Western perspective of children's place in the world). Immediately surrounding the child is the *microsystem*, or the child's day-to-day activities, settings, and encounters with social partners, such as siblings, caregivers, and teachers. At the *mesosystem* level are the connections between the different primary settings in which human development occurs. For example, children's experiences at school shape their experiences outside school, and vice versa. Besides these primary contexts, children are involved with people and institutions with which they do not immediately interact, which Bronfenbrenner termed the *exosystem*. Components of the exosystem include the local school board along with parents' workplace and network of friends. The *macrosystem*, the broader cultural contexts that shape values, beliefs, and customs, envelops these other three systems. Lastly, the *chronosystem* is the historical circumstances shaping a child's development. Research grounded in ecological systems theory focuses on how all these layers impact human development.

The ecological model applies not only to physical environments but digital and hybrid spaces as well (Takeuchi and Levine, in press; Wang et al. 2010). More is known about how children interact with parents and siblings around traditional media (like books and television) than through new media (such as virtual worlds and social networking services) (Grimes and Fields 2012). There has been a growing focus among digital media and learning researchers concerning the relationship between children's immediate social contexts and broader "media ecologies" (Horst, Herr-Stephenson, and Robinson 2010, 30). Drawing on sociocultural approaches to child development and learning sciences (Cole 1996; Bruner 1986; Rogoff 2003; Vygotsky 1978), Brigid

Barron (2004, 2006) also extends Bronfenbrenner's notion of the mesosystem through a "learning ecology" framework, which posits that children's learning is linked across multiple mediated and unmediated contexts (Barron et al. 2009).

Ecological research on media in the social lives of children also increasingly revolves around *joint media engagement* (JME), which refers to "spontaneous and designed experiences of people using media together, and can happen anywhere and at any time when there are multiple people interacting together with media" (Stevens and Penuel 2010; see also Takeuchi and Stevens 2011). JME builds on existing television-centered work on "coviewing" (Nathanson 1999; Valkenburg et al. 1999). On an average day, parents in the United States report spending about an hour using media with their children ages two to ten, with nearly fifty of those sixty minutes taken up with joint television viewing. Younger children are more likely than older ones to use media together with their caregivers (Rideout 2014). JME drops off significantly for US children around age six (Wartella et al. 2013).

Parents name various reasons why they do or do not use media together with their child. Among parents who report JME as something they do "often" or "sometimes" with their child, the leading motivations are to protect children from inappropriate content, and because the child requested that the parent watch or engage in the media activity with them (Rideout 2014). Time is a significant factor among parents who do not or rarely use media with their children. This is particularly pronounced for parents of young children, who unsurprisingly report that the time their child is occupied with media is precious time to get things done (e.g., take a shower or pay bills) (Guernsey 2012).

Beyond these initial insights, existing ecological research on children's social uses of media is limited in a number of ways.

It is unclear what kinds of content on various platforms draws children and their social partners together as well as the nature of these social interactions. Research on JME is usually limited to parent reports, and thus omits children's joint media use with peers in locations without parents (e.g., school buses or friends' homes) (Takeuchi and Levine, in press). It is also unclear how race, ethnicity, socioeconomic status, and disability status influence differences in joint media use across households. Vicky Rideout (2014) reports that while Hispanic-Latino parents spend more time than white and black parents using mobile devices with their children, time spent jointly engaging in media does not vary based on a family's racial background, income, or parent education level. The remainder of the chapter outlines existing research on the ways that family members and peers serve as social partners for the media use of youth with various disabilities, and future directions for continued inquiry.

### Parents, Caregivers, and Siblings as Social Partners

#### Parents and Caregivers

Media use can be a valued ritual among parents and youth with disabilities. Cheryl Wright and her colleagues (2011) conducted a qualitative study of Google's SketchUp 3-D modeling application among autistic boys, and discovered that it promoted communication with their parents and grandparents. Ignacio David Acevedo-Polakovich, Elizabeth Pugzles Lorch, and Richard Milich (2007) found that parents of preschool- and elementary-school-age children with ADHD were significantly more likely than parents of children without ADHD to report that their child watches television with at least one adult present in the room. Families of children with disabilities can enjoy and benefit from shared consumption and creative appropriation of specific media content (Suskind 2014). For example, in her ethnographic study of low-income black children with significant disabilities and chronic illnesses, Mattingly (2003, 2006) found that the narratives and characters in children's film and television provided rich material for children and their families to socially construct personal identities as a form of resistance against stigmatizing labels. Popular culture can become an important means of building family culture.

Parent-child JME may differ in various ways between youth with and without disabilities. Melissa Kuo and her colleagues (in press) observe that autistic adolescents frequently watch television with their parents, whereas typically developing adolescents tend to coview more with friends. They also found that autistic adolescents who watched television with their parents reported more positive parent-child relationships than autistic adolescents who did not report watching television with their parents. While it is difficult to determine causality between JME and parent-child relationships among youth with disabilities without additional information (e.g., family media rules and types of content), these findings indicate the need for further research.

It should also be stated that it is not realistic, or beneficial, to expect parents and caregivers of children with disabilities to always share in their child's media use. Youth with disabilities should have their autonomy and independence respected. Kids with disabilities may choose screen media use as a leisure activity because it is an area in which they can feel successful independently (Minihan, Fitch, and Must 2007). Some children may require assistance from their parents in order to navigate computers, and this balancing act between independent and guided use can be a source of tension between youth with disabilities and their parents (Dawe 2006). In a large-scale survey, parents of children with Down syndrome indicated that their teenage children got discouraged if they felt their parents hovering over them and violating their privacy (Feng et al. 2010). JME can potentially be intrusive depending on the child, context, and media activity.

In addition to issues of children's agency, time factors into the perceived benefits of JME among youth with disabilities and their caregivers. The parents of young people with Down syndrome in the aforementioned survey expressed concerns about their child's online safety, but also felt that they didn't have the time to closely monitor their child's activities online (Feng et al. 2010). The time that a child spends entertained by television or a mobile device may also be an opportunity for parents to take a break, find some peace and quiet, catch up on other household responsibilities, or spend time with one another without interruption (Maul and Singer 2009).

While child development experts generally revile televisions in children's bedrooms, youth with disabilities and their parents may find it helpful for children to have easy access to media that they can navigate on their own. According to parental reports, preschool- and elementary-school-age children with ADHD are nearly twice as likely to have a television in their bedroom than children without ADHD (Acevedo-Polakovich, Lorch, and Milich 2007). One explanation is that having a television in the bedroom, from the perspective of the child and parent, may help a child with ADHD cope with significant sleep difficulties. The little research that exists on parent-child JME among youth with various disabilities and their caregivers suggests that assumptions drawn from studies of typically developing children do not necessarily hold true in this case.

## Siblings

JME among siblings is disproportionately understudied considering the frequency with which it happens (Haefner, Metts, and Wartella 1989; Wilson and Weiss 1993). Based on parent reports, typically developing children ages two to ten who use screen media are more likely to frequently engage in media use with their siblings (48 percent) than with their parents (43 percent) (Rideout 2014). Video game play is a particularly social form of media use among siblings in terms of collaborative play, but also with respect to discussing game content and strategy. Game play can set the stage for spontaneous teaching and learning between siblings (Stevens, Satwicz, and McCarthy 2008).

There has been little research on joint media use among children with disabilities and their siblings. In a qualitative study of digital game play among children with physical disabilities, Amit Pitaru (2008) details how one boy valued playing *WWF Smackdown!* with his able-bodied brother because it was an activity that both could enjoy (versus playing baseball outside), utilize to compete against one another in single-player mode, and collaborate on when playing together against the computer. Through interviews with blind and visually impaired children ages eight to thirteen in Singapore, Meng Ee Wong and Libby Cohen (2011) found that their brothers and sisters often helped them to use the computer at home for various purposes (e.g., game play and homework), especially when the family computer lacked special assistive software to aid individuals with visual impairments. Considering the complex relationship between JME and cultural brokering (Correa 2014; Correa et al., in press; Katz 2010, 2014), future JME research should explore how siblings of youth with disabilities translate knowledge of digital media and assistive technologies for parents who might not be as comfortable with or aware of technology. Such research could inform how to design technologies that might encourage JME among youth with various disabilities and their family members.

## Peers, Social Media, and Social Networking Sites

Networked communication technologies can help build and maintain intimate relationships among young people, enable the coordination of social gatherings, and help define a sense of self and group identity (Livingstone 2002). These technologies currently include text messages and other messaging services (e.g., Snapchat), blogs (e.g., Tumblr), video-sharing sites (e.g., YouTube), and social networking sites (e.g., Facebook). Some of these new media technologies afford alternatives modes of peer social interaction for youth with disabilities. Asynchronous communication, for example, offers youth with cognitive disabilities more control over the pace of conversation than face-to-face or real-time mediated communication. Communicating via text or visual imagery (e.g., Instagram) does not require vocalization or hearing for youth with communication impairments or deaf youth. Online communication does not necessitate attention to neurotypical facial cues, bodily gestures, and nonverbal expressions, which some autistic youth may have difficulty interpreting.

Studies on how young people with disabilities use information and communication technologies for social purposes are generally scarce and small in scale (Pitaru 2008; Söderström and Ytterhus 2010; Näslund and Gardelli 2013), although a couple trends are apparent. First, young people with disabilities' online activities and off-line relationships are interrelated in complex ways. For instance, the results of a survey of 215 Swedish youth with physical disabilities indicated a positive association between Internet use (to email and visit online communities) and meeting friends in person (Lidström, Ahlsten, and Hemmingsson 2011). In a qualitative study of Norwegian youth ages fifteen to twenty with mobility and visual impairments, Sylvia Söderström (2009) found that most had little contact with classmates outside school, and many sought social ties online with those outside their local community. The strongest of these ties were with long-distances friends made at gatherings for disabled youth (e.g., summer camp). These relationships provide youth with the opportunity to share common experiences and recognition not found among local nondisabled peers.

Second, while youth generally value mobile phones for enabling connections to social networks, such technology may be especially important for providing a sense of security and safety for young people with disabilities (Dawe 2006). Söderström (2011) conducted a comparative study of mobile phone usage among nondisabled youth and youth with mobility disabilities, ages sixteen to twenty. Qualitative interviews shed light on how mobile phones function as a "safety net" for disabled youth. This perceived property of the phone enables a greater sense of security, increased comfort in exploring new spaces, and more flexibility in making spontaneous plans to meet up with others. The communication and social networking practices of youth with disabilities are shaped by their perceptions of the risks encountered in everyday life as well as the usefulness of information and communication technologies in reducing these risks.

Lastly, social and digital exclusion are deeply intertwined for marginalized individuals of various ages (Livingstone and Helsper 2007; Norris 2001; Selwyn 2004; Warschauer 2003). Children with physical, developmental, intellectual, emotional, and sensory disabilities are more likely to be bullied than their typically developing peers (Twyman et al. 2010). This harassment also takes the form of cyberbullying (Didden et al. 2009; Kowalski and Fedina 2011). Likely related to such harassment, Söderström (2009) discovered that many youth with mobility and visual impairments kept their disability status concealed online. They also did not visit disability-related online support groups and networks as frequently as adults with disabilities. Among adult populations with disabilities, older and newer forms of media have been, and continue to be, powerful means of forging community, storytelling, sharing resources, and organizing collective action among individuals with disabilities (Bakardjieva and Smith 2001; Cole et al. 2011; Thoreau 2006). In light of these age-related differences, without more research, it should not be assumed that youth with disabilities use information and communication technologies for social purposes among peers and other nonfamily members in the same manner as adults with disabilities (Näslund and Gardelli 2013).

## Summary

In the twenty-first century, it is difficult to find some aspect of the social lives of young people that is not in some way mediated. For better and worse, information and communication technologies shape the environments within which children learn and grow, parents work and manage their personal lives, and family members spend time with one another. In order to understand how media can support societal participation among all children, we need to better understand how youth with disabilities use media together with friends, family, and other social partners, both around and through these objects and platforms.

As cultural historians of family media use have uncovered, information and communication technologies have always been envisioned as both social and antisocial forces in children's lives. While youth with disabilities are often stereotyped as being socially isolated, the ways in which their connections with others are mediated through television, video games, mobile phones, and social media—embedded within broader media and learning ecologies—suggest a much more complex story, largely yet to be told. Chapter 4 more closely examines the new media marketplace that youth with various disabilities and their families encounter.

Commercial culture plays a significant role in Western parenting and childhood (Seiter 1995; Pugh 2009). Families of children with disabilities represent a small but growing market within the children's media industry over the last fifteen years (Canedy 1997). The products directed at parents of children with disabilities are marketed as having educational, entertainment, and therapeutic value. Consider a few recent examples: the *Toys"R"Us Toy Guide for Differently-Abled Kids*; the Common Sense Media advice brochure *Power Up! Apps for Kids with Special Needs and Learning Differences*; and "autism-friendly" or "sensory-friendly" musical performances on Broadway along with monthly movies offered by AMC Theatres. Many of these products are available online, which can be helpful for families that find it challenging to travel to a physical toy store. These organizations and companies present parents of children with disabilities (at least those who can afford to partake) with a wider array of media and technology choices than ever before.

While there are any number of blogs and Pinterest pages that offer product suggestions, my focus in this chapter is not on making specific recommendations, since what media are "best" depends on each child. Rather, I take a step back and discuss the state of this media landscape as well as issues that parents of youth with specific disabilities may encounter in selecting digital media for their child and managing their child's engagement with media. First, I provide a brief overview of the existing research on how youth with ADHD and autism are using media in their day-to-day lives. Second, I delve into the issue of what makes children's media "age appropriate." Third, I look at how determining "quality" media content for youth (both with and without disabilities) should also take into account how youth with disabilities are represented in (and missing from) popular media. Lastly, I raise issues surrounding the accessibility of information and communication technologies that are popular among children and families, like YouTube. Beyond taking children's preferences and needs into account, I argue that what media makes a best "fit" for a particular child with a disability also involves critical awareness of the limits of existing standards, content, and platforms.

## Differences across Disabilities

Youth naturally vary in their media use patterns. Children's individual needs and personal preferences influence their technology choices, habits, and routines. With regard to differences in children's media use across disabilities, a good deal of research is outdated (Gadow and Sprafkin 1993). Over just the past five years, there has been growth in scholarship on information and communication technologies use among children with intellectual disabilities (Bunning, Heath, and Minnion 2009; Mazurek et al. 2012; Palmer et al. 2012; Näslund and Gardelli 2013), Down syndrome (Al Otaiba et al. 2009; Feng et al. 2008, 2010; Oates et al. 2011), and physical disabilities (Lidström, Ahlsten, and

Hemmingsson 2011; Maher, Kernot, and Olds 2013). The following section summarizes published research on how children with ADHD and autistic children in particular use new media and technology in their everyday lives.

## ADHD

There have been a number of studies that report on the relationship between playing video games and diagnoses of ADHD. This research tends to make broad claims for such small sample sizes. For example, Philip Chan and Terry Rabinowitz (2006) found a "significant association" between playing console or online video games for more than one hour a day and "intense symptoms of ADHD" among adolescents. Nevertheless, among a sample of seventy-two ninth- and tenth-grade students, their study only included two children (both males) actually diagnosed with either attention deficit disorder or ADHD. Studies that make claims about the relationship between video game play and youth with ADHD frequently operationalize "attention problems" by screening children using ADHD symptom self-report scales or through teacher reports, not through confirmed diagnoses (see, for example, Gentile et al. 2012; Swing et al. 2010).

While research on the effects of video games is headline grabbing, it can detract from more positive findings about the media use of children diagnosed with ADHD. Parents of preschool- and elementary-school-age children with ADHD, for instance, are more likely than parents of children without ADHD to report that their child is involved in activities associated with television programs, such as playing television-related games, pretending to be television characters, and talking about television (Acevedo-Polakovich, Lorch, and Milich 2007). These findings suggest underexplored opportunities for children's literacy development through remixing and experimenting with media elements (Dyson 1997; Kinder 1991).

## Autism

There has been a recent proliferation of mainstream mobile device applications available in the Google Play and Apple iTunes App Store promoted as being designed to support learning among autistic youth (Kientz et al. 2013; Shane et al. 2012). Part of this trend stems from published research and anecdotal commentary over the past two decades suggesting many autistic people have strong visual-spatial skills (see, for instance, Grandin 1996; Quill 1997). It is unclear how these skills relate to autistic children's media habits. For example, parents report that their autistic children have strong skills in navigating interfaces for controlling media selections, particularly forwarding and rewinding videos (Nally, Houlton, and Ralph 2000; Shane and Albert 2008).

The explanation for these preferences and behaviors is not apparent, but there are a number of possible directions. Children may appreciate the chance to demonstrate self-sufficiency through making media choices and view their technical skills as a sort of personal "superpower" (Ajala 2014). Some autistic children may find that viewing and reviewing animated content is a pleasurable as well as calming form of visual self-stimulation (Shane and Albert 2008). Repeated viewing can also allow for a sense of sameness that some autistic youth report finding satisfying in software programs (Williams et al. 2002).

Compared to quantitative studies, there is a scarcity of qualitative research that explores how autistic youth use screen media in their everyday life (Kientz et al. 2013). Survey-based studies with parents have shown that autistic youth prefer to spend their free time with media. This includes watching television and movies (Nally, Houlton, and Ralph 2000; Shane and Albert 2008), and in terms of content, favoring animation (including animated television programs, DVDs, software, and character Web sites) (Lahm 1996; Shane and Albert 2008). Research points to a tendency among autistic children to spend time with visual media (e.g., television and video games) more frequently (Mazurek et al. 2012; Must et al. 2014; Orsmond and Kuo 2011) and at younger ages (Chonchaiya, Nuntnarumit, and Pruksananonda 2011) compared to typically developing children. Other research suggests that autistic youth ages thirteen to seventeen tend to spend more time with television and video games, and less time with social media (e.g., email or chat) than children their age with other disabilities (speech/language impairments, learning disabilities, or intellectual disabilities) (Mazurek et al. 2012). While there are differences in terms of media use between autistic children and their peers, there are also similarities. A large survey of parents of autistic boys ages eight to eighteen, for example, indicated that these youth are just as likely as the general population of children in the United States and Europe to have access to screen-based media in their bedrooms (Engelhardt and Mazurek 2014).

The popular claim that children with autism are "naturally" drawn to technology is open to debate (Wei et al. 2013). Most research on how autistic youth engage with electronic screen media is conducted in an experimental lab setting or based on parent reports instead of direct observation (see, for example, Mineo et al. 2009). Another problem with the claim that autistic youth are "natural techies" is that it obscures the ways in which constructions of gender shape public understandings of autism and norms around technology use (Jack 2014). Girls are underdiagnosed with autism, and there is also a huge gender gap in opportunities to gain technological expertise. Considering the ubiquity of the assertion that autistic youth have an innate attraction to technology, we know surprisingly little about how autistic youth use information and communication technologies in their lives outside school.

### How Appropriate Is Age Appropriate?

Assumptions about the relationship between specific disabilities and children's information and communication technologies use should also be examined against beliefs about what make certain media age appropriate for young people. Toys, television shows, and video games tend to have some indication of the age group for which the product is intended (e.g., TV-Y7 or PG-13). Age appropriate recommendations are grounded in research on typically developing young people's physical, social, emotional, cognitive, language, and motor development. For example, toys that potentially pose a choking hazard to children who explore the world by putting things in their mouths and whose windpipes are easily blocked are usually labeled as being for those age three and older.

Content ratings are based on certain developmental criteria that may or may not apply to a child with a disability. Media content that benefits some children of certain biological ages may not be useful to "exceptional children," or those who differ from a perceived developmental norm.[1] For example, Howard Shane and Patti Albert (2008) found that parents of autistic youth ages eighteen and younger indicated that the most popular television character for this population is Winnie the Pooh, and the most popular Web site is PBSkids.com. These media tend to be marketed to young audiences. What makes media appropriate for youth with disabilities is not strictly determined by the biological age of the child. It is important to note too, though, that age appropriateness needs to be considered to some extent so as not to eliminate inclusive social opportunities with same-biological age peers (chapter 3).

Even those products specifically designed for youth with disabilities have shortcomings. Many educational apps targeting children with disabilities are of poor quality, and have not undergone research as part of their design and development. Educational software programs that might best support the academic skills of older children with learning and intellectual disabilities are often designed for much younger children, use pictures of young children, and have childish voices (Feng et al. 2010; Näslund and Gardelli 2013). Children with motor impairments who require simpler interfaces for video game play frequently have difficulty finding content that is also cognitively challenging (Pitaru 2008). While there may be more media options available to younger children with disabilities than at any other point in history, it is important to keep in mind that their media preferences will change as they grow up too.

### Misrepresenting Disability in Children's Media

Media content should also be evaluated for how it excludes or misrepresents disabled individuals. People with disabilities are the largest minority in the world and yet are the most underrepresented in entertainment media. Out of the 796 characters regularly appearing on scripted shows on major television networks in 2013, only 8 (or 1 percent) had disabilities (GLAAD 2014). While contemporary mainstream media created for child audiences (including books, movies, and television shows) increasingly include positive representations of disability (Haller 2010; Millett 2004), the portrayal of youth with disabilities in children's media is still disproportionately low and lacks diversity (Golos 2010; Hardin et al. 2001; Leininger et al. 2010). Emiliano Ayala (1999), for example, found that while children's literature in the twenty years following IDEA's passage portrayed a greater array of disabilities, few books contained ethnically, culturally, or linguistically diverse disabled characters.

Oversights and misrepresentations of media characters from historically underrepresented groups have implications for all children (Berry and Asamen 1993). Inaccurate, negative, and altogether-absent media portrayals of people with disabilities shape how children with and without disabilities conceptualize disability (Curwood 2013). More recently, young adult novels such as *Wonder* by R. J. Palacio and *Out of My Mind* by Sharon Draper have addressed the complex dynamics of inclusive education and depicted young people with disabilities as directly confronting antidisability discrimination (Wheeler 2013). Beyond representation, it is crucial for children of all abilities to see rich, complex characters not defined solely by their disability and included as a natural part of society.

### Inaccessible by Design

Young people and their caregivers can only judge and evaluate media content that is made available to them. Inaccessible platforms, applications, and Web sites strongly discourage individuals with disabilities from cultural as well as societal participation (Ellis and Kent 2010; Goggin and Newell 2003). Rapid iterations and frequent changes to existing digital media products and services can have unintended impacts on user accessibility (Goggin

2008). Pitaru (2008, 75) demonstrated that upgrades to video games were sources of anxiety among youth with disabilities, who worried about such "improvements" negatively impacting accessibility. When upgraded operating systems and platforms do not support existing software, new compatible software is only available to children if software companies decide to release such versions. Buying entirely new software can be cost prohibitive for parents and schools. Even with adaptive input devices and controllers, most mainstream video games are inaccessible in a number of ways for youth with physical, sensory, and cognitive disabilities (Yuan, Folmer, and Harris 2011). Difficulties navigating inaccessible digital media can deter spontaneous, independent play among youth with disabilities as well as collaborative play with parents, siblings, and friends.

In addition to gaming, online video is another medium that can pose a challenge to youth with disabilities. Online video is made more accessible for deaf and hard-of-hearing individuals through closed-captioning, an alternative textual language translation of a video's primary audio language. Hearing users can also benefit from closed-captioning, such as when watching television in a loud gym or bar. Research has shown that for typically developing beginning readers, closed-captioning can be an effective form of literacy support (Linebarger, Piotrowski, and Greenwood 2009).Closed-captioning can also streamline translation for online video content into multiple languages. This is particularly vital for YouTube, where 80 percent of the views come from outside the United States (Ellis 2013).

Closed-captioning can be generally helpful in a number of ways for people with and without disabilities—at least when it works. YouTube's auto-captioning is notoriously poor, and offers no way for deaf and hard-of-hearing YouTube users to search exclusively for videos with proper captioning (Lockrey 2013). The US Twenty-First Century Communications and Video Accessibility Act mandated that as of October 2013, all new video programming shown on the Internet, after being broadcast on television, must have captions. But the act excluded video programming exclusively distributed via the Internet (e.g., YouTube and Vimeo videos). To fill in the gaps, a number of volunteer-driven crowdsourcing technologies such as Amara.org have emerged to improve captioning and video descriptions at little or no cost to content creators and distributors (Ellcessor 2010)

These efforts have met with resistance from industry forces, however, which contend that the creation or improvement of captioning without the express permission of a video's copyright holder violates the Digital Millennium Copyright Act (Telecommunications for the Deaf and Hard of Hearing, Inc. 2011). Though the Federal Communications Commission (2013) expects content distributors, publishers, and owners to voluntarily caption online video clips, there are no guarantees that this will actually happen in the near future. In fact, in February 2014, California's Ninth Circuit Court of Appeals ruled that CNN (and its parent company, Time Warner) be allowed to forego video captioning when delivering and reporting the news on its Web sites. The court ruled on the grounds that the potential delays and costs of captioning would impinge on CNN's free speech rights (Gardner 2014). While California's Disabled Persons Act entitles citizens to "full and equal access" to public spaces, it has yet to be determined if Web sites legally count as places of "general accommodation." Such a ruling would impact the extent to which deaf and hard-of-hearing youth can take part in online activities.

How digital tools and online spaces are designed and built at least in part determines who can and cannot participate in our networked society. This is not to say that assistive hardware and software are inherently beneficial to young people. Assistive technologies that improve access to new media can also be socially stigmatizing as well as symbolize dependency and weakness, and thus ultimately youth may avoid them (Wielandt et al. 2006). This is particularly true of adolescents and teenagers with disabilities desiring to "fit in" with their peers. For example, Sylvia Söderström and Borgunn Ytterhus (2010) found in interviews with partially sighted youth in Norway that they avoided using a screen reader to access the Web and play computer games because they associated the tool with standing out—an identity deviant from their peer culture. Meanwhile, in the same study, blind youth valued text-to-speech software that made "ordinary" technologies like mobile phones accessible and allowed them to maintain their privacy while communicating with friends. The extent to which accessibility options are rejected or embraced by youth with different disabilities is shaped by a number of factors, including how visibly the technology marks youth as "different" and how necessary it is to participating in peer communities.

## Summary

Children have unique preferences and needs, and these are important to take into account when analyzing the wide range of media and technology that exists for children with disabilities to use. Besides these individual factors, though, young people, parents, and caregivers should be aware of more systematic issues that shape how content is made available to children, which media and technology are suggested to parents of children with disabilities, and why the characters in popular media are constructed in certain ways. It is not clear-cut what makes media appropriate or inappropriate for children of different ages, especially when taking into account youth with disabilities.

# 5 Conclusion

The main aim of this report has been to make a case for broadening common perceptions about who is counted among digital youth. I have brought together a wide range of research across disciplines (e.g., communication, sociology, anthropology, and human-computer interaction) on how youth with disabilities adopt and use media at home as well as part of their household activities. I have placed terms that dominate the conversation about children and media in the United States—such as screen time (chapter 2) and age-appropriate media (chapter 4)—under the metaphoric microscope to examine the assumptions about children and ability on which these ideas are based. Chapter 3 captures how disability is a dynamic factor shaping how families relate to media, one another, and society at large. The remainder of this report outlines clear parameters for future research on the experiences that youth with disabilities and their families have with media in the age of digital, mobile, and networked technologies.

## Areas for Future Research and Development

### Connected Learning

More research is needed on how learning that takes place through media use at home might be leveraged across the different social settings (e.g., school, clubs, and community groups) in which youth with disabilities learn. This encompasses a range of physical, digital, and more hybrid spaces. According to the "connected learning" framework (Ito et al. 2013), learning is most successful when it is reinforced in multiple contexts and embedded within a strong network of social relationships, can support young people's interest-driven learning, and that learning can be directed toward traditional educational, economic, and political opportunities. Intergenerational partnerships, mentoring programs, and learning communities can be particularly impactful for young people with disabilities.

### Social Media Use

Parents need carefully vetted information on the social benefits and drawbacks of specific types of information and communication technologies for children with various disabilities. For example, little is known about young people with disabilities' engagement in virtual worlds (Stendal 2012). While there has been some research done on how texting can be a crucial mode of communication for deaf and hard-of-hearing youth, little is known about their use of other increasingly popular mobile platforms such as Snapchat and Instagram. In addition to mainstream social network sites, there is much to be learned about young people's sociality within online communities specific to various disabilities, including Squag, a social networking site for autistic children, and Asperclick, a site founded by a young woman with Asperger's syndrome.

### Market Analysis

Snapshots of the children's digital media industry are helpful tools for tracking trends along with holding the developers of apps, software, Web sites, and games accountable to their educational claims (see, for example, Guernsey et al. 2012). At present, there has been no substantial evaluation of the rapidly growing special education category in Apple's iTunes App Store, which showcases some of the most expensive apps in the entire App Store. While changes in technology are swift, it is important to understand how this market is evolving and if parents are being taken advantage of.

### Active Video Gaming

Youth with disabilities are at a higher risk of childhood obesity than typically developing children (chapter 2). Among typically developing youth, there have been mixed results regarding whether or not active video games or "exergames" (e.g., Wii Fit) can increase overall physical activity levels. Outside rehabilitation settings, there is limited research on the casual use of active video games among children with physical or cognitive disabilities (Biddiss and Irwin 2010). Motion-sensing devices such as the Kinect for Xbox may be particularly helpful for use at home because they are easily customizable and can provide individualized feedback through the games.

### Creative Computing

A number of technologies for creative production are designed in ways that take into account natural variation in how children learn, play, move, and think. These include Scratch, a visual programming environment (Resnick and Silverman 2005), and MaKey MaKey, a tangible interface that can be used to adapt previously inaccessible technology such as video game controllers (Silver, Rosenbaum, and Shaw 2012). Little is known, however, about how youth with disabilities and their families make use of these technologies (Leduc-Mills, Dec, and Schimmel 2013; Peppler and Warschauer 2012).

## Multiple Dimensions of Difference

While we know that diverse populations of young people have taken up digital media (Everett 2008b), it is unclear how race, ethnicity, gender, sexuality, and class factor into the use (and nonuse) of digital media by youth with different disabilities. For example, Peg Lindstrand (2002) found that parents of children with disabilities reported having gendered expectations of their child's interest in computer-based activities, resulting in more limited opportunities with technology for girls with disabilities. More work is also needed on activist work by youth with disabilities, and how this work is facilitated by networked communication technologies and digital media.

## Summary

Young people with disabilities are not waiting idly for others' permission to use new media in interesting and unexpected ways. As they have been historically, youth with disabilities are drivers of technological change, media makers, and innovators themselves (see, for instance, Lang 2000). Many are taking part in Kickstarter and Change.org campaigns, hosting their own YouTube channels, exploring animation and filmmaking, and creating Tumblr sites showcasing their creative endeavors (see, for example, DiBlasio 2014; NBC News 2014). As with other young people, they engage in friendship- and interest-driven uses of media outside the classroom, laboratory, and therapeutic setting (Ito et al. 2009).

While advances in media and technology have enabled a wider range of possibilities among youth with disabilities, these options exist among various institutional, educational, cultural, economic, and social constraints. As Mizuko Ito and her colleagues (2013, 41) write, "Without a broader vision of social change, ... new technologies will only serve to reinforce existing institutional goals and forms of social inequity." Young people with disabilities are at great risk for being isolated from educational, economic, and political opportunities, preventing them from competing and contributing as adults with disabilities in the twenty-first century and beyond. Because so many of the quickly evolving technologies we interact with every day are lacking applied research, finding and exploring the factors underlying how media shapes and is shaped by learning communities of those with disabilities is key.

# Appendix: Additional Resources on Digital Media and Youth with Disabilities

### General

*AbleGamers*: http://www.ablegamers.com

*DIY Ability*: http://diyability.org

*Media dis&dat* (Beth Haller): http://media-dis-n-dat.blogspot.com

*Tech Kids Unlimited*: http://www.techkidsunlimited.org

### Cerebral Palsy

*Love That Max* (Ellen Seidman): http://www.lovethatmax.com

### Autism

*The iQ Journals* (Melissa Morgenlander): http://www.iqjournals.com

*Squidalicious* (Shannon Rosa): http://www.squidalicious.com

*University of Edinburgh DART (Development Autism Research Technology)*: http://www.dart.ed.ac.uk

### Media Projects by Youth with Disabilities

*Aaronverse* (Aaron Philip): http://aaronverse.tumblr.com

*EmpoweredFeFes* (Access Living, Chicago): http://www.accessliving.org/index.php?tray=topic&tid=118gatop22&cid=118ga294

# Notes

## 1  Introduction

1. This report covers research published on the use of home media by youth with disabilities ages three to twenty-two. While that age range is wider and older than most work concentrating on digital youth, it reflects young people's eligibility to receive special education and related services in the United States under the Individuals with Disabilities Education Act (IDEA). In addition, since literature on the casual use of media and technology by youth with disabilities is so scarce, casting a wide net reveals more areas in which inquiry is needed among children of various ages. Though focused on the United States in scope, this report also draws on relevant work conducted by researchers in Europe. For a more global perspective on theoretical approaches and studies into the lived experiences of children with disabilities, see Curran and Runswick-Cole 2013.

2. Since October 2012, I have been conducting fieldwork for my dissertation. This research includes home observations and interviews with parents of children with developmental disabilities. A number of examples in the report reflect my experience working with this population. I have also interviewed teachers, therapists, and staff members of nonprofit organizations in the Los Angeles area who serve the needs of children with various disabilities about their experiences with media and technology in the classroom as well as therapeutic settings. In the past few years, I have attended seminars through the Assistive Technology

Institute and Junior Blind of America, and taken a class in assistive technology through the University of Southern California's Department of Occupational Science and Occupational Therapy. The report has also benefited from my participation on conference panels and in workshops, and collaboration with Professor Kylie Peppler as special education media arts reviewers of the National Coalition for Core Arts Standards through the John F. Kennedy Center for the Performing Arts.

3. This includes children educated at correctional facilities, homes, hospitals, public and private schools, and residential facilities.

4. The category labeled other health impairment is difficult to summarize, as it includes a number of disabilities and disorders. IDEA defines it as "having limited strength, vitality, or alertness, including a heightened alertness to environmental stimuli, that results in limited alertness with respect to the educational environment, that—(i) Is due to chronic or acute health problems such as asthma, attention deficit disorder or attention deficit hyperactivity disorder, diabetes, epilepsy, a heart condition, hemophilia, lead poisoning, leukemia, nephritis, rheumatic fever, sickle cell anemia, and Tourette syndrome; and (ii) Adversely affects a child's educational performance" (US Government Printing Office n.d.).

5. The ADA, the 1990 civil rights law that protects the equal rights of all people with disabilities, presents another definition of a *person with a disability*. This definition includes a person who has a physical or mental impairment that substantially limits one or more of their major life activities, a history or record of such an impairment, or is perceived by others as having such an impairment.

6. It is also crucial to note, though, that there have been tensions between parents of children with disabilities and adults with disabilities, who sometimes feel that parents often overshadow their own voices in society (Stevenson, Harp, and Gernsbacher 2011).

## 2 The Trouble with Screen Time

1. This definition of screen time is not to be confused with its more common meaning: the time allotted to an actor or actress on film or television.

2. Though the AAP's (1999, 342) policy statement in 1999 on media education advises pediatricians to encourage parents to limit their child's "time spent with media," the term screen time does not appear until the AAP's follow-up policy statement in 2001.

3. Prior to the CCFC's involvement, the Center for SCREEN-TIME Awareness (formerly the TV-Turnoff Network, and earlier, TV-Free America) coordinated Screen-Free Week, which began as "TV-Turnoff Week" in 1994.

4. While not covered in this report, the effect of media on the violent behavior of youth with disabilities is also a growing concern among researchers (see, for example, Mazurek and Engelhardt 2013a, 2013b).

## 3 Youth Sociality through and around Media

1. Some human development scholars have critiqued children's media researchers referencing "Bronfenbrenner's ecological theory" for not citing this model in its most mature form (Tudge et al. 2009). Urie Bronfenbrenner's (2005) full theory of human development consists of the "Process-Person-Context-Time," or PPCT model. The microsystem, mesosystem, ecosystem, macrosystem, and chronosystem comprise the *context*, which is interrelated with the other three PPCT concepts. *Process* is the enduring dynamic relationship between individuals and their environments over a life span. *Person* is the individual's biological, genetic, cognitive, emotional, and physical characteristics. Bronfenbrenner also subdivided *time* into three levels: *microtime* (the course of an interaction or activity), *mesotime* (the frequency and consistency of these activities and interactions in a person's life), and *macrotime* (the current point in chronological history).

## 4 Evaluating Children's Media

1. The term exceptional children is inclusive of children with disabilities as well as children who are intellectually gifted and talented—categories that are not mutually exclusive (e.g., a child with dyslexia who is gifted at math).

# References

AAP (American Academy of Pediatrics). 1988. "Commercialization of Children's Television and Its Effect on Imaginative Play." *Pediatrics* 81:900–901.

AAP (American Academy of Pediatrics). 1990. "Children, Adolescents, and Television." *Pediatrics* 85:1119–1120.

AAP (American Academy of Pediatrics). 1999. "Media Education." *Pediatrics* 104, no. 2:341–343.

AAP (American Academy of Pediatrics). 2001. "Media Violence." *Pediatrics* 108, no. 5:1222–1226.

AAP (American Academy of Pediatrics). 2010. "Children, Adolescents, Substance Abuse, and the Media." *Pediatrics* 126, no. 4:791–799.

AAP (American Academy of Pediatrics). 2011. "Children, Adolescents, Obesity, and the Media." *Pediatrics* 128, no. 1:201–208.

AAP (American Academy of Pediatrics). 2013. "Children, Adolescents, and the Media." *Pediatrics* 132, no. 5:958–961.

AAP (American Academy of Pediatrics). n.d. Media and Children. http://www.aap.org/en-us/advocacy-and-policy/aap-health-initiatives/Pages/Media-and-Children.aspx (accessed on April 26, 2014).

Acevedo-Polakovich, I. D., E. P. Lorch, and R. Milich. 2007. "Comparing Television Use and Reading in Children with ADHD and Non-Referred Children across Two Age Groups." *Media Psychology* 9, no. 2:447–472.

Acevedo-Polakovich, I. D., E. P. Lorch, R. Milich, and R. D. Ashby. 2006. "Disentangling the Relation between Television Viewing and Cognitive Processes in Children with Attention-Deficit/Hyperactivity Disorder and Comparison Children." *Archives of Pediatrics and Adolescent Medicine* 160, no. 4:354–360.

Adams, R. 2013. *Raising Henry: A Memoir of Motherhood, Disability, and Discovery*. New Haven, CT: Yale University Press.

Adkins, B., J. Summerville, M. Knox, A. R. Brown, and S. Dillon. 2013. "Digital Technologies and Musical Participation for People with Intellectual Disabilities." *New Media and Society* 15, no. 4:501–518.

Adorno, T., and M. Horkheimer. 2002. *Dialectic of Enlightenment*. Palo Alto, CA: Stanford University Press.

Ajala, F. 2014. "Superpower." *Perspectives*. KQED Public Radio, San Francisco, January 30. http://www.kqed.org/a/perspectives/R201401300735 (accessed on April 30, 2014).

Al Otaiba, S., S. Lewis, K. Whalon, A. Dyrlund, and A. R. McKenzie. 2009. "Home Literacy Environments of Young Children with Down Syndrome: Findings from a Web-Based Survey." *Remedial and Special Education* 30, no. 2:96–107.

Alper, M. 2013. "Children and Convergence Culture." In *The Routledge International Handbook of Children, Adolescents, and Media*, ed. D. Lemish, 148–155. London: Routledge.

Alper, M., J. P. Hourcade, and S. Gilutz. 2012. "Interactive Technologies for Children with Special Needs." In *Proceedings of the International Conference on Interaction Design and Children (IDC), Bremen, Germany, June 12–15*, 363–366. New York: ACM.

Appadurai, A. 1996. *Modernity at Large: Cultural Dimensions of Globalization*. Minneapolis: University of Minnesota Press.

Aud, S., S. Wilkinson-Flicker, P. Kristapovich, A. Rathbun, and X. Wang. 2013. *The Condition of Education 2013*. NCES 2013–037. Washington, DC: US Department of Education, National Center for Education Statistics. http://nces.ed.gov/pubs2013/2013037.pdf (accessed on June 6, 2014).

Ayala, E. C. 1999. "'Poor Little Things' and 'Brave Little Souls': The Portrayal of Individuals with Disabilities in Children's Literature." *Reading Research and Instruction* 39, no. 1:103–117.

Bakardjieva, M., and R. Smith. 2001. "The Internet in Everyday Life." *New Media and Society* 3:67–83.

Bakken, F. 2005. "SMS Use among Deaf Teens and Young Adults in Norway." In *The Inside Text: Social, Cultural, and Design Perspectives on SMS*, ed. R. Harper, L. Palen, and A. Taylor, 161–174. Amsterdam: Springer.

Balsamo, A. 1995. *Technologies of the Gendered Body: Reading Cyborg Women*. Durham, NC: Duke University Press.

Barron, B. 2004. "Learning Ecologies for Technological Fluency: Gender and Experience Differences." *Journal of Educational Computing Research* 31, no. 1:1–36.

Barron, B. 2006. "Interest and Self-Sustained Learning as Catalysts of Development: A Learning Ecology Perspective." *Human Development* 49:193–224.

Barron, B., C. K. Martin, L. Takeuchi, and R. Fithian. 2009. "Parents as Learning Partners in the Development of Technological Fluency." *International Journal of Learning and Media* 1, no. 2:55–77.

Barsch, R. H. 1961. "Explanations Offered by Parents and Siblings of Brain-Damaged Children." *Exceptional Children* 27:286–291.

Belcher, C., and B. Herr-Stephenson. 2011. *Teaching Harry Potter: The Power of Imagination in Multicultural Classrooms*. New York: Palgrave Macmillan.

Benjamin, W. 1968. "The Work of Art in the Age of Mechanical Reproduction." In *Illuminations*, trans. H. Arendt, 217–251. New York: Schocken.

Bernheimer, L. P., R. Gallimore, and T. S. Weisner. 1990. "Ecocultural Theory as a Context for the Individual Family Service Plan." *Journal of Early Intervention* 14:219–233.

Berry, G. L., and J. K. Asamen. 1993. *Children and Television: Images in a Changing Sociocultural World.* London: Sage.

Biddiss, E., and J. Irwin. 2010. "Active Video Games to Promote Physical Activity in Children and Youth: A Systematic Review." *Archives of Pediatrics and Adolescent Medicine* 164, no. 7:664–672.

Borchert, M. 1998. "The Challenge of Cyberspace: Internet Access and Persons with Disabilities." In *Cyberghetto or Cybertopia: Race, Class, and Gender on the Internet*, ed. B. Ebo, 45–64. Westport, CT: Praeger.

Bouck, E. C., C. M. Okolo, and C. A. Courtad. 2007. "Technology at Home: Implications for Children with Disabilities." *Journal of Special Education Technology* 22, no. 3:43–56.

Bovill, M., and S. Livingstone. 2001. "Bedroom Culture and the Privatization of Media Use." In *Children and Their Changing Media Environment: A European Comparative Study*, ed. S. Livingstone and M. Bovill, 179–200. Mahwah, NJ: Erlbaum.

boyd, d. 2014. *It's Complicated: The Social Lives of Networked Teens.* New Haven, CT: Yale University Press.

Boyle, C. A., S. Boulet, L. A. Schieve, R. A. Cohen, S. J. Blumberg, M. Yeargin-Allsopp, S. Visser, and M. D. Kogan. 2011. "Trends in the Prevalence of Developmental Disabilities in U.S. Children, 1997–2008." *Pediatrics* 127, no. 6:1034–1042.

Bradbury, R. 1950. "The World the Children Made (The Veldt)." *Saturday Evening Post*, September 23.

Bronfenbrenner, U. 1979. *The Ecology of Human Development.* Cambridge, MA: Harvard University Press.

Bronfenbrenner, U. 1986. "Ecology of the Family as a Context for Human Development: Research Perspectives." *Developmental Psychology* 22, no. 6:723–742.

Bronfenbrenner, U. 2005. *Making Human Beings Human: Bioecological Perspectives on Human Development*. Thousand Oaks, CA: Sage.

Brown, L. 2011. "The Significance of Semantics: Person-First Language: Why It Matters." *Autistic Hoya* (blog), August 4, http://www.autistic hoya.com/2011/08/significance-of-semantics-person-first.html (accessed on April 21, 2014).

Bruner, J. 1986. *Actual Minds, Possible Worlds*. Cambridge, MA: Harvard University Press.

Buckingham, D. 1993. *Children Talking Television: The Making of Television Literacy*. London: Falmer.

Buckingham, D. 2006. "Children and New Media." In *Handbook of New Media: Social Shaping and Social Consequences*, ed. L. Lievrouw and S. Livingstone, 75–91. London: Sage.

Buckingham, D., and J. Sefton-Green. 1997. "From Regulation to Education." *English and Media Magazine* 36:28–32.

Bunning, K., B. Heath, and A. Minnion. 2009. "Communication and Empowerment: A Place for Rich and Multiple Media?" *Journal of Applied Research in Intellectual Disabilities* 22:370–379.

Burman, E. 2001. "Beyond the Baby and the Bathwater: Postdualistic Developmental Psychologies for Diverse Childhoods." *European Early Childhood Education Research Journal* 9, no. 1:5–22.

Burman, E. 2008. *Deconstructing Developmental Psychology*. London: Routledge.

Butler, J. 1990. *Gender Trouble: Feminism and the Subversion of Identity*. New York: Routledge.

Candey, D. 1997. "More Toys Are Reflecting Disabled Children's Needs." *New York Times*, December 25. http://www.nytimes.com/1997/12/25/business/more-toys-are-reflecting-disabled-children-s-needs.html (accessed on April 30, 2014).

Cannon, K. L., and J. M. Barker. 2012. "Hard Candy." In *Moving Data: The iPhone and the Future of Media*, ed. P. Snickars and P. Vonderau, 73–88. New York: Columbia University Press.

Carr, N. 2010. *The Shallows: What the Internet Is Doing to Our Brains*. New York: W. W. Norton.

Cassell, J., and M. Cramer. 2008. "High Tech or High Risk: Moral Panics about Girls Online." In *Digital Youth, Innovation, and the Unexpected*, ed. T. McPherson, 53–76. Cambridge, MA: MIT Press.

CCFC (Campaign for a Commercial Free Childhood). 2013. Media advisory, April 25. Boston, MA: Campaign for a Commercial Free Childhood. http://www.screenfree.org/press.html (accessed on April 27, 2014).

Chan, P. A., and T. Rabinowitz. 2006. "A Cross-Sectional Analysis of Video Games and Attention Deficit Hyperactivity Disorder Symptoms in Adolescents." *Annals of General Psychiatry* 5, no. 16. http://www.annals -general-psychiatry.com/content/5/1/16 (accessed on June 6, 2014).

Charlton, J. I. 2000. *Nothing about Us without Us: Disability Oppression and Empowerment*. Berkeley: University of California Press.

Chonchaiya, W., P. Nuntnarumit, and C. Pruksananonda. 2011. "Comparison of Television Viewing between Children with Autism Spectrum Disorder and Controls." *Acta Paediatrica* 100:1033–1037.

Christakis, D. A., F. J. Zimmerman, D. L. DiGiuseppe, and C. A. McCarty. 2004. "Early Television Exposure and Subsequent Attentional Problems in Children." *Pediatrics* 113, no. 4:708–713.

Clark, L. S. 2013. *The Parent App: Understanding Families in the Digital Age*. New York: Oxford University Press.

Clarke, J. N. 2012. "Representations of Autism in US Magazines for Women in Comparison to the General Audience." *Journal of Children and Media* 6, no. 2:182–197.

Cohen, C., and J. Kahne, with B. Bowyer, E. Middaugh, and J. Rogowski. 2012. *Participatory Politics: New Media and Youth Political Action*. Chicago: John D. and Catherine T. MacArthur Foundation.

Cohen, S. 1972. *Folk Devils and Moral Panics: The Creation of the Mods and Rockers*. London: MacGibbon and Kee.

Cole, J., J. Nolan, Y. Seko, K. Mancuso, and A. Ospinanal. 2011. "Gimp-Girl Grows Up: Women with Disabilities Rethinking, Redefining, and Reclaiming Community." *New Media and Society* 13, no. 7:1161–1179.

Cole, M. 1996. *Cultural Psychology: A Once and Future Discipline*. Cambridge, MA: Harvard University Press.

Coontz, S. 1992. *The Way We Never Were: American Families and the Nostalgia Trap*. New York: Basic Books.

Cooper, H. 2013. "The Oppressive Power of Normalcy in the Lives of Disabled Children: Deploying History to Denaturalize the Notion of the 'Normal' Child." In *Disabled Children's Childhood Studies: Critical Approaches in a Global Context*, ed. T. Curran and K. Runswick-Cole, 136–151. New York: Palgrave Macmillan.

Correa, T. 2014 "Bottom-Up Technology Transmission within Families: Exploring How Youths Influence Their Parents' Digital Media Use with Dyadic Data." *Journal of Communication* 64, no. 1:103–124.

Correa, T., J. D. Straubhaar, W. Chen, and J. Spence. In press. "Brokering New Technologies: The Role of Children in Their Parents' Usage of the Internet." *New Media and Society*. http://nms.sagepub.com/content/early/2013/10/15/1461444813506975.abstract (accessed July 27, 2014).

Curran, T., and K. Runswick-Cole, eds. 2013. *Disabled Children's Childhood Studies: Critical Approaches in a Global Context*. New York: Palgrave Macmillan.

Curwood, J. S. 2013. "Redefining Normal: A Critical Analysis of (Dis)ability in Young Adult Literature." *Children's Literature in Education* 44:15–28.

Davis, L. J. 1995. *Enforcing Normalcy: Disability, Deafness, and the Body*. London: Verso.

Dawe, M. 2006. "Desperately Seeking Simplicity: How Young Adults with Cognitive Disabilities and Their Families Adopt Assistive Technologies." In *Proceedings of the SIGCHI Conference on Human Factors in Computing Systems*, 1143–1152. New York: ACM.

DeGusta, M. 2012. Are Smart Phones Spreading Faster than Any Technology in Human History? *MIT Technology Review*, May 9. http://www.technologyreview.com/news/427787/are-smart-phones-spreading-faster-than-any-technology-in-human-history (accessed on April 27, 2014).

Dell, A. G., D. Newton, and J. G. Petroff. 2011. *Assistive Technology in the Classroom: Enhancing the School Experiences of Students with disabilities.* 2nd ed. Upper Saddle River, NJ: Pearson.

DiBlasio, N. 2014. "10-Year-Old Petitions for Disabled American Girl Doll." *USA Today*, January 2. http://www.usatoday.com/story/news/nation/2014/01/02/american-girl-disabled-doll/4287897 (accessed on May 2, 2014).

Didden, R., R.H.J. Scholte, H. Korzilius, J. M. De Moor, A. Vermeulen, M. O'Reilly, R. Lang, and G. E. Lancioni. 2009. "Cyberbullying among Students with Intellectual and Developmental Disability in Special Education Settings." *Developmental Neurorehabilitation* 12, no. 3:146–151.

Dobransky, K., and E. Hargittai. 2006. "The Disability Divide in Internet Access and Use." *Information Communication and Society* 9, no. 3:313–334.

Doheny, K. 2010. Too Much Screen Time Can Threaten Attention Span. *U.S. News and World Report*, July 5. http://health.usnews.com/health-news/family-health/brain-and-behavior/articles/2010/07/05/too-much-screen-time-can-threaten-attention-span (accessed on April 26, 2014).

Downer, M. L. 1957. "'FRIGHTENING STATISTIC' CITED. Curb Urged on Time Spent by Youngsters Viewing TV." *Los Angeles Times*, March 3, E10.

Durkin, K., and G. Conti-Ramsden. 2014. "Turn Off or Tune In? What Advice Can SLTs, Educational Psychologists and Teachers Provide about Uses of New Media and Children with Language Impairments?" *Child Language Teaching and Therapy* 30, no. 2:187–205.

Dyson, A. H. 1997. *Writing Superheroes: Contemporary Childhood, Popular Culture, and Classroom Literacy*. New York: Teachers College Press.

Dyson, A. H. 2003. *The Brothers and Sisters Learn to Write: Popular Literacies in Childhood and School Cultures*. New York: Teachers College Press.

Ellcessor, E. 2010. "Bridging Disability Divides." *Information Communication and Society* 13, no. 3:289–308.

Ellis, B. 2013. "Best Practices for Implementing Accessible Video Captioning." Paper presented at the Streaming Media West Conference, November 13. http://www.3playmedia.com/how-it-works/webinars/best-practices-implementing-accessible-video-captioning-11-19-2013/ (accessed on May 1, 2014).

Ellis, K., and M. Kent. 2010. *Disability and New Media*. New York: Routledge.

Engelhardt, C. R., and M. O. Mazurek. 2014. "Video Game Access, Parental Rules, and Problem Behavior: A Study of Boys with Autism Spectrum Disorder." *Autism* 30, no. 2:187–205.

Engelhardt, C. R., M. O. Mazurek, and K. Sohl. 2014. "Media Use and Sleep among Boys with Autism Spectrum Disorder, ADHD, or Typical Development." *Pediatrics*. http://pediatrics.aappublications.org/content/early/2013/11/12/peds.2013-2066.abstract (accessed July 27, 2014).

Everett, A. 2008a. Introduction to *Learning Race and Ethnicity: Youth and Digital Media*, ed. A. Everett, 1–14. Cambridge, MA: MIT Press.

Everett, A., ed. 2008b. *Learning Race and Ethnicity: Youth and Digital Media*. Cambridge, MA: MIT Press.

Federal Communications Commission. 2013. "Order on Reconsideration and Further Notice of Proposed Rulemaking before the Federal Communications Commission in the Matter of Closed Captioning of Internet Protocol—Delivered Video Programming: Implementation of the Twenty-First Century Communications and Video Accessibility Act of 2010 (MB Docket No. 11–154)." http://transition.fcc.gov/Daily_Releases/Daily_Business/2013/db0614/FCC-13-84A1.pdf (accessed on May 2, 2014).

Feng, J., J. Lazar, L. Kumin, and A. Ozok. 2008. "Computer Usage by Young Individuals with Down Syndrome: An Exploratory Study." In *Proceedings of the 10th International ACM SIGACCESS Conference on Computers and Accessibility*, 35–42. New York: ACM.

Feng, J., J. Lazar, L. Kumin, and A. Ozok. 2010. "Computer Usage by Children with Down Syndrome: Challenges and Future Research." *ACM Transactions on Accessible Computing* 2, no. 3: article 13.

Fleishmann, A., and C. Fleishmann. 2012. *Carly's Voice: Breaking through Autism*. New York: Touchstone.

Flichy, P. 2006. "New Media History." In *Handbook of New Media: Social Shaping and Social Consequences*, ed. L. Lievrouw and S. Livingstone, 187–204. London: Sage.

Ford, D. Y. 2012. "Culturally Different Students in Special Education: Looking Backward to Move Forward." *Exceptional Children* 78, no. 4:391–405.

Foucault, M. 1973. *The Birth of the Clinic: An Archeology of Medical Perception*. New York: Vintage.

Fox, S. 2011. *Americans Living with Disability and Their Technology Profile*. Washington, DC: Pew Research Center's Internet and American Life Project. http://www.pewInternet.org/~/media//Files/Reports/2011/PIP_ Disability.pdf (accessed on April 21, 2014).

Gadow, K. D., and J. Sprafkin. 1993. "Television 'Violence' and Children with Emotional and Behavioral Disorders." *Journal of Emotional and Behavioral Disorders* 1, no. 1:54–63.

Gardner, E. 2014. "CNN Gets First Amendment Victory in Video Captioning Dispute." *Hollywood Reporter*, February 5. http://www.holly woodreporter.com/thr-esq/cnn-gets-first-amendment-victory-677446 (accessed on May 2, 2014).

Garland Thomson, R. 1996. *Extraordinary Bodies: Figuring Physical Disability in American Culture and Literature*. New York: Columbia University Press.

Garrison, M. M., K. Liekweg, and D. A. Christakis. 2011. "Media Use and Child Sleep: The Impact of Content, Timing, and Environment." *Pediatrics* 128, no. 1:29–35.

Gentile, D. A., E. L. Swing, C. G. Lim, and A. Khoo. 2012. "Video Game Playing, Attention Problems, and Impulsiveness: Evidence of Bidirectional Causality." *Psychology of Popular Media Culture* 1, no. 1:62–70.

Gill, C. J. 1995. "A Psychological View of Disability Culture." *Disability Studies Quarterly* 15, no. 4: 16–19.

Ginsburg, F., L. Abu-Lughod, and B. Larkin, eds. 2002. *Media Worlds: Anthropology on New Terrain.* Berkeley: University of California Press.

GLAAD. 2014. "Where We Are on TV Report 2013." Los Angeles, CA: GLAAD. http://www.glaad.org/files/2013WWATV.pdf (accessed on May 1, 2014).

Goggin, G. 2008. "Innovation and Disability." *M/C Journal* 11, no. 3. http://journal.media-culture.org.au/index.php/mcjournal/article/view/56 (accessed on May 1, 2014).

Goggin, G., and C. Newell. 2003. *Digital Disability: The Social Construction of Disability in New Media.* Lanham, MD: Rowman and Littlefield.

Golos, D. B. 2010. "The Representation of Deaf Characters in Children's Educational Television in the U.S." *Journal of Children and Media* 4, no. 3:248–264.

Goodley, D., and K. Runswick-Cole. 2010. "Emancipating Play: Dis/abled Children, Development, and Deconstruction." *Disability and Society* 25, no. 4:499–512.

Grandin, T. 1996. *Thinking in Pictures and Other Reports from My Life.* New York: Vintage.

Green, S. E. 2003. "What Do You Mean 'What's Wrong with Her?': Stigma and the Lives of Families of Children with Disabilities." *Social Science and Medicine* 57, no. 8:1361–1374.

Grimes, S. M., and D. A. Fields. 2012. *Kids Online: A New Research Agenda for Understanding Social Networking Forums*. New York: Joan Ganz Cooney Center at Sesame Workshop.

Guernsey, L. 2012. *Screen Time: How Electronic Media—from Baby Videos to Educational Software—Affects Your Young Child*. New York: Basic Books.

Guernsey, L. 2014. "Garbled in Translation: Getting Media Research to the Press and Public." *Journal of Children and Media* 8, no. 1:87–94.

Guernsey, L., M. Levine, C. Chiong, and M. Severns. 2012. *Pioneering Literacy in the Digital Wild West: Empowering Parents and Educators*. New York: Joan Ganz Cooney Center at Sesame Workshop.

Guha, M. L., A. Druin, and J. A. Fails. 2008. "Designing with and for Children with Special Needs: An Inclusionary Model." In *IDC '08 Proceedings of the 7th International Conference on Interaction Design and Children*, 61–64. New York: ACM.

Haefner, M. J., S. Metts, and E. Wartella. 1989. "Siblings' Strategies for Resolving Conflict over Television Program Choice." *Communication Quarterly* 37, no. 3:223–230.

Hager, E. 2010. "IPad Opens World to a Disabled Boy." *New York Times*, October 31, LI8.

Halfon, N., A. Houtrow, K. Larson, and P. W. Newacheck. 2012. "The Changing Landscape of Disability in Childhood." *Future of Children* 22, no. 1:13–42.

Haller, B. A. 2010. *Representing Disability: Essays on Mass Media*. Louisville, KY: Advocado Press.

Hardin, B., M. Hardin, S. Lynn, and K. Walsdorf. 2001. "Missing in Action? Images of Disability in *Sports Illustrated for Kids*." *Disability Studies Quarterly* 21, no. 2. http://dsq-sds.org/article/view/277/303 (accessed on June 6, 2014).

Hayes, G. R., S. Hirano, G. Marcu, M. Monibi, D. H. Nguyen, and M. Yeganyan. 2010. "Interactive Visual Supports for Children with Autism." *Personal and Ubiquitous Computing* 14, no. 7:663–680.

Hays, S. 1996. *The Cultural Contradictions of Motherhood*. New Haven, CT: Yale University Press.

Hendershot, H. 1998. *Saturday Morning Censors: Television Regulation before the V-Chip*. Durham, NC: Duke University Press.

Hendershot, H. 2004. *Nickelodeon Nation*. New York: New York University Press.

Hochschild, A. R. 1983. *The Managed Heart: The Commercialization of Human Feeling*. Berkeley: University of California Press.

Hochschild, A. R. 1989. *The Second Shift: Working Parents and the Revolution at Home*. New York: Viking Penguin.

Hochschild, A. R. 1997. *The Time Bind: When Work Becomes Home and Home Becomes Work*. New York: Henry Holt.

Hoover, S., L. S. Clark, and D. Alters. 2004. *Media, Home, and Family*. New York: Routledge.

Hornik, R. C. 1981. "Out-of-School Television and Schooling: Hypotheses and Methods." *Review of Educational Research* 51:199–214.

Horst, H. A., B. Herr-Stephenson, and L. Robinson. 2010. "Media Ecologies." In *"Hanging Out, Messing Around, and Geeking Out: Kids Living and Learning with New Media,"* ed. M. Ito, S. Baumer, M. Bittanti, d. boyd, R. Cody, B. Herr-Stephenson, H. A. Horst, et al., 29–78. Cambridge, MA: MIT Press.

Ito, M., S. Baumer, M. Bittanti, d. boyd, R. Cody, B. Herr-Stephenson, H. A. Horst, P. G. Lange, D. Mahendran, K. Z. Martinez, C. J. Pascoe, D. Perkel, L. Robinson, C. Sims, and L. Tripp. 2009. *Hanging Out, Messing around, Geeking Out: Living and Learning with New Media*. Cambridge, MA: MIT Press.

Ito, M., K. Gutiérrez, S. Livingstone, B. Penuel, J. Rhodes, K. Salen, J. Schor, J. Sefton-Green, and S. C. Watkins. 2013. *"Connected Learning: An Agenda for Research and Design*. Irvine, CA: Digital Media and Learning Research Hub.

Jack, J. 2014. *Autism and Gender: From Refrigerator Mothers to Computer Geeks.* Champaign: University of Illinois Press.

James, A., and A. Prout, eds. 1997. *Constructing and Reconstructing Childhood: Contemporary Issues in the Sociological Study of Childhood.* Philadelphia: RoutledgeFarmer.

Jenkins, H. 1998. "Introduction: Childhood Innocence and Other Modern Myths." In *The Children's Culture Reader,* ed. H. Jenkins, 1–37. New York: New York University Press.

Jenkins, H. 2006. *Convergence Culture: Where Old and New Media Collide.* New York: New York University Press.

Jenkins, H., with R. Purushotma, K. Clinton, M. Weigel, and A. J. Robison. 2006. *Confronting the Challenges of Participatory Culture: Media Education for the 21st Century.* Chicago: John D. and Catherine T. MacArthur Foundation.

Johnson, S. 2005. *Everything Bad Is Good for You: How Today's Popular Culture Is Actually Making Us Smarter.* New York: Penguin.

Jordan, A. 1992. "Social Class, Temporal Orientation, and Mass Media Use within the Family System." *Critical Studies in Media Communication* 9:374–386.

Jordan, A. 2004. "The Role of Media in Children's Development: An Ecological Perspective." *Developmental and Behavioral Pediatrics* 25, no. 3:196–206.

Kafer, A. 2013. *Feminist, Queer, Crip.* Bloomington: Indiana University Press.

Kaneshiro, N. K. 2011. "Screen Time and Children." *Medline Plus.* Washington, DC: National Institutes of Health, July 1. http://www.nlm.nih.gov/medlineplus/ency/patientinstructions/000355.htm (accessed on April 27, 2014).

Katz, V. S. 2010. "How Children of Immigrants Use Media to Connect Their Families to the Community." *Journal of Children and Media* 4, no. 3:298–315.

Katz, V. S. 2014. *Kids in the Middle: How Children of Immigrants Negotiate Community Interactions for Their Families*. New Brunswick, NJ: Rutgers University Press.

Keilty, B., and K. M. Galvin. 2006. "Physical and Social Adaptations of Families to Promote Learning in Everyday Experiences." *Topics in Early Childhood Special Education* 26, no. 4:219–233.

Kientz, J. A., M. S. Goodwin, G. R. Hayes, and G. D. Abowd. 2013. *Interactive Technologies for Autism*. San Rafael, CA: Morgan and Claypool.

Kinder, M. 1991. *Playing with Power in Movies, Television, and Video Games: From Muppet Babies to Teenage Mutant Ninja Turtles*. Berkeley: University of California Press.

King-Sears, M. E., C. Swanson, and L. Mainzer. 2011. "TECHnology and Literacy for Adolescents with Disabilities." *Journal of Adolescent and Adult Literacy* 54, no. 8:569–578.

Kirkpatrick, B. 2012. "'A Blessed Boon': Radio, Disability, Governmentality, and the Discourse of the 'Shut-In,' 1920–1930." *Critical Studies in Media Communication* 29, no. 3:165–184.

Kleeman, D. 2010. "'A Screen Is a Screen Is a Screen' Is a Meme." *Huffington Post*, December 8. http://www.huffingtonpost.com/david -kleeman/a-screen-is-a-screen-is-a_b_792742.html (accessed on April 27, 2014).

Kleeman, D. 2012. "Going 'Screen Free' vs. Going 'Screen Smart.'" *Huffington Post*, April 30. http://www.huffingtonpost.com/david-kleeman/ screen-free-week_b_1462177.html (accessed on April 27, 2014).

Kowalski, R. W., and C. Fedina. 2011. "Cyber Bullying in ADHD and Asperger Syndrome Populations." *Research in Autism Spectrum Disorders* 5, no. 3:1201–1208.

Krcmar, M. 2009. *Living without the Screen: Causes and Consequences of Life without Television*. London: Routledge.

Kuo, M. H., G. I. Orsmond, W. J. Coster, and E. S. Cohn. In press. "Media Use among Adolescents with Autism Spectrum Disorder" *Autism*. http://

aut.sagepub.com/content/early/2013/10/18/1362361313497832
.abstract (accessed on July 26, 2014).

Lahm, E. 1996. "Software That Engages Young Children with Disabilities: A Study of Design Features." *Focus on Autism and Other Developmental Disabilities* 11, no. 2:115–124.

Landsman, G. H. 2009. *Reconstructing Motherhood and Disability in the Age of "Perfect" Babies.* New York: Routledge.

Lang, H. G. 2000. *A Phone of Our Own: The Deaf Insurrection against Ma Bell.* Washington, DC: Gallaudet University Press.

Lapsley, P. 2013. *Exploding the Phone: The Untold Story of the Teenagers and Outlaws Who Hacked Ma Bell.* New York: Grove Press.

Lareau, A. 2000. *Home Advantage: Social Class and Parental Intervention in Elementary Education.* Oxford: Rowman and Littlefield.

Leduc-Mills, B., J. Dec, and J. Schimmel. 2013. "Evaluating Accessibility in Fabrication Tools for Children." In *IDC '13 Proceedings of the 12th International Conference on Interaction Design and Children,* 617–620. New York: ACM.

Leininger, M., T. T. Dyches, M. A. Prater, and M. A. Heath. 2010. "Newbery Award Winning Books, 1975–2009: How Do They Portray Disabilities?" *Education and Training in Autism and Developmental Disabilities* 45, no. 4:583–596.

Lewin, T. 2011. Screen Time Higher than Ever for Children. *New York Times,* October 25. http://www.nytimes.com/2011/10/25/us/screen -time-higher-than-ever-for-children-study-finds.html (accessed on April 26, 2014).

Lhamon, C. E., and J. Samuels. 2014. *Dear Colleague Letter on the Nondiscriminatory Administration of School Discipline.* Washington, DC: US Department of Justice, Civil Rights Division, and US Department of Education, Office for Civil Rights, January 8. http://www2.ed.gov/ about/offices/list/ocr/letters/colleague-201401-title-vi.pdf (accessed on April 24, 2014).

Lidström, H., G. Ahlsten, and H. Hemmingsson. 2011. "The Influence of ICT on the Activity Patterns of Children with Physical Disabilities outside School." *Child: Care, Health, and Development* 37, no. 3:313–321.

Lin, S. C., S. M. Yu, and R. L. Harwood. 2012. "Autism Spectrum Disorders and Developmental Disabilities in Children from Immigrant Families in the United States." *Pediatrics* 13 (Supplement 2): S191–S197.

Lindstrand, P. 2002. "Pleasure or Utility? Different Conditions for Boys and Girls with Disabilities in Information and Communication Technology." *International Journal of Rehabilitation Research* 25, no. 1:9–16.

Linebarger, D., J. T. Piotrowski, and C. R. Greenwood. 2009. "On-Screen Print: The Role of Captions as a Supplemental Literacy Tool." *Journal of Research in Reading* 33, no. 2:148–167.

Linton, S. 1998. *Claiming Disability.* New York: New York University Press.

Liususan, A.W.L., L. T. Abresch, and C. M. McDonald. 2004. "Altered Body Composition Affects Resting Energy Expenditure: Interpretation of Body Mass Index in Children with Spinal Cord Injury." *Journal of Spinal Cord Medicine* 27 (Supplement 1): S24–S28.

Livingstone, S. 2002. *Young People and New Media.* London: Sage.

Livingstone, S., and E. Helsper. 2007. "Gradations in Digital Inclusion: Children, Young People, and the Digital Divide." *New Media and Society* 9, no. 4:671–696.

Lo, C. B. 2013. "The Effects of Family and Social Engagement on the Screen Time of Youth with Developmental Disabilities: A Dissertation." PhD diss., University of Massachusetts Medical School. http://escholarship.umassmed.edu/gsbs_diss/658 (accessed on April 28, 2014).

Lockrey, M. 2013. "Opinion: The Scourge of You-Tube's Auto-Captions." *Media Access Australia* (blog), April 10. shttp://mediaaccess.org.au/latest_news/general/opinion-the-scourge-of-youtube's-auto-caption (accessed on May 2, 2014).

Longmore, P. 2013. "'Heaven's Special Child': The Making of Poster Children." In *The Disability Studies Reader*, ed. L. J. Davis, 34–41. 4th ed. New York: Routledge.

Longmore, P., and L. Umansky, eds. 2001. *The New Disability History: American Perspectives*. New York: New York University Press.

Lin, S. C., S. M. Yu, and R. L. Harwood. 2012. "Autism Spectrum Disorders and Developmental Disabilities in Children from Immigrant Families in the United States." *Pediatrics* 13 (Supplement 2): S191–S197.

Linton, S. 1998. *Claiming Disability: Knowledge and Identity*. New York: New York University Press.

Lull, J. 1990. *Inside Family Viewing: Ethnographic Research on Television's Audiences*. New York: Routledge.

Maccoby, E. 1951. "Television: Its Impact on School Children." *Public Opinion Quarterly* 32:102–112.

Madden, M., A. Lenhart, M. Duggan, S. Cortesi, and U. Gasser. 2013. *Teens and Technology, 2013*. Washington, DC: Pew Research Center's Internet and American Life Project.

Maher, C., J. Kernot, and T. Olds. 2013. "Time Use Patterns in Ambulatory Adolescents with Cerebral Palsy." *Child: Care, Health, and Development* 39, no. 3:404–411.

Marvin, C. 1998. *When Old Technologies Were New: Thinking about Electric Communications in the Late Nineteenth Century*. New York: Routledge.

Mattingly, C. 2003. "Becoming Buzz Lightyear and Other Clinical Tales: Indigenizing Disney in a World of Disability." *Folk* 45:9–32.

Mattingly, C. 2006. "Pocahontas Goes to the Clinic: Popular Culture as Lingua Franca in a Cultural Borderland." *American Anthropologist* 108, no. 3:494–501.

Maul, C. A., and G. H. S. Singer. 2009. "'Just Good Different Things': Specific Accommodations Families Make to Positively Adapt to Their Children with Developmental Disabilities." *Topics in Early Childhood Special Education* 29, no. 3:155–170.

Mazurek, M. O., and C. R. Engelhardt. 2013a. "Video Game Use and Problem Behaviors in Boys with Autism Spectrum Disorders." *Research in Autism Spectrum Disorders* 7:316–324.

Mazurek, M. O., and C. R. Engelhardt. 2013b. "Video Game Use in Boys with Autism Spectrum Disorder, ADHD, or Typical Development." *Pediatrics* 132:260–266.

Mazurek, M. O., P. T. Shattuck, M. Wagner, and B. P. Cooper. 2012. "Prevalence and Correlates of Screen-Based Media Use among Youths with Autism Spectrum Disorders." *Journal of Autism and Developmental Disorders* 42:1757–1767.

McPherson, M., P. Arango, H. Fox, C. Lauver, M. McManus, P. Newacheck, J. Perrin, J. Shonkoff, and B. Strickland. 1998. "A New Definition of Children with Special Health Care Needs." *Pediatrics* 102, no. 1:137–140.

McRuer, R. 2006. *Crip Theory: Cultural Signs of Queerness and Disability.* New York: New York University Press.

Metzel, D. S., and P. M. Walker. 2001. "The Illusion of Inclusion: Geographies of the Lives of People with Developmental Disabilities in the United States." *Disability Studies Quarterly* 21, no. 4:114–128.

Milich, R., and E. P. Lorch. 1994. "Television Viewing Methodology to Understand Cognitive Processing of ADHD Children." In *Advances in Clinical Child Psychology*, ed. T. H. Ollendick and R. J. Prinz, 177–201. Vol. 16. New York: Plenum.

Milich, R., E. P. Lorch, and K. S. Berthiaume. 2005. "Story Comprehension in Children with ADHD: Research Findings and Treatment Implications." In *Attention Deficit Hyperactivity Disorder Research*, ed. M. P. Larimer, 111–136. Hauppauge, NY: Nova Science.

Millett, A. 2004. "'Other' Fish in the Sea: 'Finding Nemo' as an Epic Representation of Disability." *Disability Studies Quarterly* 24, no. 1. http:// dsq-sds.org/article/view/873/1048 (accessed on May 1, 2014).

Mineo, B. A., W. Ziegler, S. Gill, and D. Salkin. 2009. "Engagement with Electronic Screen Media among Students with Autism Spectrum Disorders." *Journal of Autism and Developmental Disorders* 39:172–187.

Minihan, P. M., S. N. Fitch, and A. Must. 2007. "What Does the Epidemic of Childhood Obesity Mean for Children with Special Health Care Needs?" *Journal of Law, Medicine, and Ethics* 35, no. 1:61–77.

Mittell, J. 2000. "The Cultural Power of an Anti-Television Metaphor: Questioning the 'Plug-In Drug' and a TV-Free America." *Television and New Media* 1, no. 2:215–238.

Moni, K. B., and A. Jobling. 2008. "A Case for Including Popular Culture in Literacy Education for Young Adults with Down Syndrome." *Australian Journal of Language and Literacy* 31, no. 3:260–277.

Morley, D. 1988. *Family Television: Cultural Power and Domestic Leisure*. New York: Routledge.

Morris, K. A., and R. J. Morris. 2006. "Disability and Juvenile Delinquency: Issues and Trends." *Disability and Society* 21, no. 6:613–627.

Moser, I. 2006. "Disability and the Promises of Technology: Technology, Subjectivity, and Embodiment within an Order of the Normal." *Information Communication and Society* 9, no. 3:373–395.

Must, A., S. M. Phillips, C. Curtin, S. E. Anderson, M. Maslin, K. Lividini, and L. G. Bandini. 2014. "Comparison of Sedentary Behaviors between Children with Autism Spectrum Disorders and Typically Developing Children." *Autism* 18, no. 4:376–384.

Mutz, D. C., D. F. Roberts, and D. P. van Vuuren. 1993. "Reconsidering the Displacement Hypothesis: Television's Influence on Children's Time Use." *Communication Research* 20, no. 1:51–75.

Nally, B., B. Houlton, and S. Ralph. 2000. "Researches in Brief: The Management of Television and Video by Parents of Children with Autism." *Autism* 4, no. 3:331–338.

Näslund, R., and Å. Gardelli. 2013. "'I Know, I Can, I Will Try': Youths and Adults with Intellectual Disabilities in Sweden Using Information and Communication Technology in Their Everyday Life." *Disability and Society* 28, no. 1:28–40.

Nathanson, A. I. 1999. "Identifying and Explaining the Relationship between Parental Mediation and Children's Aggression." *Communication Research* 26, no. 2:124–143.

NBC News. 2014. "Boy with Cerebral Palsy Inspires with Tumblr Blog." *TODAY*, January 7. http://www.today.com/video/today/54002948#5400 2948 (accessed on May 2, 2014).

Newman, M. Z. 2010. "New Media, Young Audiences, and Discourses of Attention: From Sesame Street to 'Snack Culture.'" *Media, Culture and Society* 32, no. 4:581–596.

Nielsen, K. E. 2012. *A Disability History of the United States*. Boston: Beacon Press.

Nippert-Eng, C. E. 1996. *Home and Work: Negotiating Boundaries through Everyday Life*. Chicago: University of Chicago Press.

Norris, P. 2001. *Digital Divide: Civic Engagement, Information Poverty, and the Internet Worldwide*. Cambridge: Cambridge University Press.

Oates, A., A. Bebbington, J. Bourke, S. Girdler, and H. Leonard. 2011. "Leisure Participation for School-Aged Children with Down Syndrome." *Disability and Rehabilitation* 33, no. 19–20:1880–1889.

Oliver, M. 1990. *The Politics of Disablement*. Basingstoke, UK: Macmillan.

Ong-Dean, C. 2009. *Distinguishing Disability: Parents, Privilege, and Special Education*. Chicago: University of Chicago Press.

Orsmond, G. I., and H. Kuo. 2011. "The Daily Lives of Adolescents with an Autism Spectrum Disorder: Discretionary Time Use and Activity Partners." *Autism* 15:1–21.

Owens, J., R. Maxim, M. McGuinn, C. Nobile, M. Msall, and A. Alario. 1999. "Television Habits and Sleep Disturbance in School Children." *Pediatrics* 104, no. 3:e27.

Palmer, S. B., M. L. Wehmeyer, D. K. Davies, and S. E. Stock. 2012. "Family Members' Reports of the Technology Use of Family Members with Intellectual and Developmental Disabilities." *Journal of Intellectual Disability Research* 56, no. 4:402–414.

Parkes, A., H. Sweeting, D. Wight, and M. Henderson. 2013. "Do Television and Electronic Games Predict Children's Psychosocial Adjustment? Longitudinal Research Using the UK Millennium Cohort Study." *Archives of Disease in Childhood* 98:341–348.

Patterson, J. M. 2002. "Integrating Family Resilience and Family Stress Theory." *Journal of Marriage and the Family* 64:349–360.

Peppler, K. A., and M. Warschauer. 2012. "Uncovering Literacies, Disrupting Stereotypes: Examining the (Dis)abilities of a Child Learning to Computer Program and Read." *International Journal of Learning and Media* 3, no. 3:15–41.

Pitaru, A. 2008. "E Is for Everyone: The Case for Inclusive Game Design." In *The Ecology of Games: Connecting Youth, Games, and Learning*, ed. K. Salen, 67–88. Cambridge, MA: MIT Press.

Pugh, A. J. 2009. *Longing and Belonging: Parents, Children, and Consumer Culture*. Berkeley: University of California Press.

Quill, K. 1997. "Instructional Considerations for Young Children with Autism: The Rationale for Visually Cued Instruction." *Journal of Autism and Developmental Disorders* 27:697–714.

Radway, J. 1984. *Reading the Romance: Women, Patriarchy, and Popular Literature*. Chapel Hill: University of North Carolina Press.

Radway, J. 1986. "Reading Is Not Eating: Mass-Produced Literature and the Theoretical, Methodological, and Political Consequences of a Metaphor." *Book Research Quarterly* 2:7–29.

Rapp, R., and F. Ginsburg. 2011. "Reverberations: Disability and the New Kinship Imaginary." *Anthropological Quarterly* 84, no. 2:379–410.

Resnick, M., and B. Silverman. 2005. "Some Reflections on Designing Construction Kits for Kids." In *IDC '05 Proceedings of the 4th International Conference on Interaction Design and Children*, 117–122. New York: ACM.

Rich, M. 2007. "Is Television Healthy? The Medical Perspective." In *Children and Television: Fifty Years of Research*, ed. N. Pecora, J. P. Murray, and E. A. Wartella, 109–147. Mahwah, NJ: Erlbaum.

Rideout, V. R. 2012. *Social Media, Social Life: How Teens View Their Digital Lives*. San Francisco: Common Sense Media.

Rideout, V. R. 2013. *Zero to Eight: Children's Media Use in America, 2013*. San Francisco: Common Sense Media.

Rideout, V. J. 2014. *Learning at Home: Families' Educational Media Use in America: A Report of the Families and Media Project*. New York: Joan Ganz Cooney Center at Sesame Workshop.

Rimmer, J. H., J. L. Rowland, and K. Yamaki. 2007. "Obesity and Secondary Conditions in Adolescents with Disabilities: Addressing the Needs of an Underserved Population." *Journal of Adolescent Health* 41, no. 3:224–229.

Rogoff, B. 2003. *The Cultural Nature of Human Development*. New York: Oxford University Press.

Rogow, F. 2013. "Why Counting Screen Time Minutes Isn't an Education Strategy." *Fred Rogers Center* (blog), October 1. http://www .fredrogerscenter.org/blog/counting-screen-time-minutes-isnt-an-educa tion-strategy (accessed on April 28, 2014).

Rosenbaum, R. 1971. "Secrets of the Little Blue Box." *Esquire* (October):117–125, 222–226.

Rosenberg, M. 1997. "To Foster Family Activities, Turn Off the TV." *New York Times*, February 2, WC13.

Safford, P. L., and E. J. Safford, eds. 2006. *Children with Disabilities in America: A Historical Handbook and Guide*. Westport, CT: Greenwood Press.

Sarachan, J. 2012. "Limiting Screen Time Is Not the Key to Parenting in the Digital Age." *International Journal of Learning and Media* 3, no. 4:1–5.

Scott, E. K. 2010. "'I Feel as if I Am the One Who Is Disabled': The Emotional Impact of Changed Employment Trajectories of Mothers Caring for Children with Disabilities." *Gender and Society* 24, no. 5:672–696.

"Screen Time Calculated." 1975. *Hartford Courant*, May 11, 19A.

Seiter, E. 1995. *Sold Separately: Parents and Children in Consumer Culture.* New Brunswick, NJ: Rutgers University Press.

Seiter, E. 1999. *Television and New Media Audiences.* Oxford: Oxford University Press.

Seiter, E. 2005. *The Internet Playground: Children's Access, Entertainment, and Mis-Education.* New York: Peter Lang.

Seiter, E. 2007. "Practicing at Home: Computers, Pianos, and Cultural Capital." In *Digital Youth, Innovation, and the Unexpected*, ed. T. McPherson, 27–52. Cambridge, MA: MIT Press.

Selwyn, N. 2004. "Reconsidering Political and Popular Understandings of the Digital Divide." *New Media and Society* 6, no. 3:341–362.

Siebers, T. 2008. *Disability Theory.* Ann Arbor: University of Michigan Press.

Silver, J., E. Rosenbaum, and D. Shaw. 2012. "MaKey MaKey: Improvising Tangible and Nature-Based User Interfaces." In *TEI '12 Proceedings of the 6th International Conference on Tangible, Embedded, and Embodied Interaction*, 367–370. New York: ACM.

Silverstone, R., and E. Hirsch, eds. 1992. *Consuming Technologies: Media and Information in Domestic Spaces.* London: Routledge.

Shakespeare, T. 2013. *Disability Rights and Wrongs Revisited.* New York: Routledge.

Shane, H. C., and P. D. Albert. 2008. "Electronic Screen Media for Persons with Autism Spectrum Disorders: Results of a Survey." *Journal of Autism and Developmental Disorders* 38:1499–1508.

Shane, H. C., E. H. Laubscher, R. W. Schlosser, S. Flynn, J. F. Sorce, and J. Abramson. 2012. "Applying Technology to Visually Support Language and Communication in Individuals with Autism Spectrum Disorders." *Journal of Autism and Developmental Disorders* 42, no. 6:1228–1235.

Shapiro, J. P. 1993. *No Pity: People with Disabilities Forging a New Civil Rights Movement*. New York: Times Books.

Shute, N. 2013. "Boys with Autism or ADHD More Prone to Overuse Video Games." *National Public Radio*, July 29. http://www.npr.org/blogs/ health/2013/07/29/206667837/boys-with-autism-or-adhd-more-prone -to-overuse-video-games (accessed on April 27, 2014).

Siebers, T. 2008. *Disability Theory*. Ann Arbor: University of Michigan Press.

Snyder, T. D., and S. A. Dillow. 2012. *Digest of Education Statistics, 2011 (NCES 2012–001)*. Washington, DC: National Center for Education Statistics, Institute of Education Sciences, US Department of Education.

Sobchack, V. 2004. "A Leg to Stand On: Prosthetics, Metaphor, and Materiality." In *Carnal Thoughts: Embodiment and Moving Image Culture*, 205–225. Berkeley: University of California Press.

Söderström, S. 2009. "Offline Social Ties and Online Use of Computers: A Study of Disabled Youth and Their Use of ICT Advances." *New Media and Society* 11, no. 5:709–727.

Söderström, S. 2011. "Staying Safe While on the Move: Exploring Differences in Disabled and Non-Disabled Young People's Perceptions of the Mobile Phone's Significance in Daily Life." *Young* 19, no. 1:91–109.

Söderström, S., and B. Ytterhus. 2010. "The Use and Non-Use of Assistive Technologies from the World of Information and Communication Technology by Visually Impaired Young People: A Walk on the Tightrope of Peer Inclusion." *Disability and Society* 25, no. 3:303–315.

Solomon, A. 2012. *Far from the Tree: Parents, Children, and the Search for Identity*. New York: Scribner.

Sousa, A. C. 2011. "From Refrigerator Mothers to Warrior-Heroes: The Cultural Identity Transformation of Mothers Raising Children with Intellectual Disabilities." *Symbolic Interaction* 34, no. 2:220–243.

Spigel, L. 1992. *Make Room for TV: Television and the Family Ideal in Post-war America*. Chicago: University of Chicago Press.

Star, S. L. 1991. "Power, Technologies, and the Phenomenology of Conventions: On Being Allergic to Onions." In *A Sociology of Monsters? Essays on Power, Technology, and Domination*, ed. J. Law, 26–56. London: Routledge.

Stendal, K. 2012. "How Do People with Disability Use and Experience Virtual Worlds and ICT: A Literature Review." *Journal of Virtual Worlds Research* 5, no. 1. http://journals.tdl.org/jvwr/index.php/jvwr/article/view/6173 (accessed on June 6, 2014).

Stern, A. M. 2005. *Eugenic Nation: Faults and Frontiers of Better Breeding in Modern America*. Berkeley: University of California Press.

Stevens, R., and W. R. Penuel. 2010. "Studying and Fostering Learning through Joint Media Engagement." Paper presented at the Principal Investigators Meeting of the National Science Foundation's Science of Learning Centers, Arlington, VA.

Stevens, R., T. Satwicz, and L. McCarthy. 2008. "In-Game, In-Room, In-World: Reconnecting Video Game Play to the Rest of Kids' Lives." In *The Ecology of Games: Connecting Youth, Games, and Learning*, ed. K. Salen, 41–68. Cambridge, MA: MIT Press.

Stevenson, J. L., B. Harp, and M. A. Gernsbacher. 2011. "Infantilizing Autism." *Disability Studies Quarterly* 31, no. 3. http://dsq-sds.org/article/view/1675/1596 (accessed April 24, 2014).

Suskind, R. 2014. "Reaching My Autistic Son through Disney." *New York Times*, March 9. http://www.nytimes.com/2014/03/09/magazine/reaching-my-autistic-son-through-disney.html (accessed on April 29, 2014).

Swing, E. L., D. A. Gentile, C. A. Anderson, and D. A. Walsh. 2010. "Television and Video Game Exposure and the Development of Attention Problems." *Pediatrics* 126:214–221.

Takeuchi, L., and M. H. Levine. 2014. "Learning in a Digital Age: Towards a New Ecology of Human Development." In *Media and the*

*Well-Being of Children and Adolescents*, ed. A. Jordan and D. Romer, 20–43. New York: Oxford University Press.

Takeuchi, L., and R. Stevens. 2011. *The New Coviewing: Designing for Learning through Joint Media Engagement*. New York: The Joan Ganz Cooney Center at Sesame Workshop.

Telecommunications for the Deaf and Hard of Hearing, Inc., Gallaudet University, and Participatory Culture Foundation. 2011. "Comments before the United States Copyright Office and the Library of Congress, in the Matter of: Exemption to Prohibition on Circumvention of Copyright Protection Systems for Access Control Technologies Notice of Inquiry and Request for Comments (Docket No. RM 2011–7)." http://www.copyright.gov/1201/2011/initial/IPR_TDI_gallaudetU.pdf (accessed on May 2, 2014).

Thompson, D. A., and D. A. Christakis. 2005. "The Association between Television Viewing and Irregular Sleep Schedules among Children Less than Three Years of Age." *Pediatrics* 116, no. 4:851–856.

Thoreau, E. 2006. "*Ouch!* An Examination of the Self-Representation of Disabled People on the Internet." *Journal of Computer-Mediated Communication* 11:442–468.

Thorne, B. 2009. "'Childhood': Changing and Dissonant Meanings." *International Journal of Learning and Media* 1, no. 1:19–27.

Trainor, A. A. 2010. "Reexamining the Promise of Parent Participation in Special Education: An Analysis of Cultural and Social Capital." *Anthropology and Education Quarterly* 41, no. 3:245–263.

Tudge, J.R.H., I. Mokrova, B. E. Hatfield, and R. B. Karnik. 2009. "Uses and Misuses of Bronfenbrenner's Bioecological Theory of Human Development." *Journal of Family Theory and Review* 1:198–210.

Turkle, S. 2011. *Alone Together: Why We Expect More from Technology and Less from Each Other*. New York: Basic Books.

Turow, J. 1981. *Entertainment, Education, and the Hard Sell: Three Decades of Network Children's Television*. New York: Praeger.

Twyman, K. A., C. F. Saylor, D. Saia, M. M. Macias, L. A. Taylor, and E. Spratt. 2010. "Bullying and Ostracism Experiences in Children with Special Health Care Needs." *Journal of Developmental and Behavioral Pediatrics* 31:1–8.

US Department of Commerce, National Telecommunications and Information Administration, and Economics and Statistics Administration. 2013. *Exploring the Digital Nation: America's Emerging Online Experience.* Washington, DC: US Department of Commerce.

US Department of Health and Human Services, Health Resources and Services Administration, Maternal and Child Health Bureau. 2013. *The National Survey of Children with Special Health Care needs Chartbook, 2009–2010.* Rockville, MD: US Department of Health and Human Services.

US Government Printing Office. n.d. Electronic Code of Federal Regulations. http://www.ecfr.gov/cgi-bin/text-idx?c=ecfr&sid=96025ad40230a e0f4a530ec51d0519ca&rgn=div5&view=text&node=34:2.1.1.1.1&i dno=34#34:2.1.1.1.1.36.7 (accessed on June 5, 2014).

Valkenburg, P. M., M. Krcmar, A. L. Peeters, and N. M. Marseille. 1999. "Developing a Scale to Assess Three Styles of Television Mediation: 'Instructive Mediation,' 'Restrictive Mediation,' and 'Social Coviewing.'" *Journal of Broadcasting and Electronic Media* 43, no. 1:52–66.

Vandewater, E. A. 2013. "Ecological Approaches to the Study of Children and Media." In *Routledge Handbook of Children, Adolescents, and Media,* ed. D. Lemish, 46–53. London: Routledge.

Vandewater, E. A., and H. M. Cummings. 2011. "Media Use and Childhood Obesity." In *Blackwell Handbook of Child Development and the Media,* ed. S. L. Calvert and B. J. Wilson, 355–380. Oxford, UK: Blackwell.

Vygotsky, L. S. 1978. *Mind in Society: The Development of Higher Psychological Processes.* Cambridge, MA: Harvard University Press.

Walkerdine, V. 1993. "Beyond Developmentalism." *Theory and Psychology* 3, no. 4:451–469.

Wang, X. C., I. R. Berson, C. Jaruszewicz, L. Hartle, and D. Rosen. 2010. "Young Children's Technology Experiences in Multiple Contexts: Bronfenbrenner's Ecological Theory Reconsidered." In *High-Tech Tots: Childhood in a Digital World*, ed. I. R. Berson and M. J. Berson, 23–47. Greenwich, CT: Information Age.

Warschauer, M. 2003. *Technology and Social Inclusion: Rethinking the Digital Divide*. Cambridge, MA: MIT Press.

Wartella, E., and B. Reeves. 1985. "Historical Trends in Research on Children and the Media: 1900–1960." *Journal of Communication* 35, no. 2:118–133.

Wartella, E., V. Rideout, A. Lauricella, and S. Connell. 2013. *Parenting in the Age of Digital Technology: A National Survey*. Evanston, IL: Center on Media and Human Development, School of Communication, Northwestern University.

Wartella, E., and M. Robb. 2008. "Historical and Recurring Concerns about Children's Use of the Mass Media." In *The Handbook of Children, Media, and Development*, ed. S. Calvert and B. Wilson, 7–26. Malden, MA: Blackwell.

Watkins, S. C. 2009. *The Young and the Digital: What the Migration to Social Network Sites, Games, and Anytime, Anywhere Media Means for Our Future*. Boston: Beacon Press.

Wei, X., J. W. Yu, P. Shattuck, M. McCracken, and J. Blackorby. 2013. "Science, Technology, Engineering, and Mathematics (STEM) Participation among College Students with an Autism Spectrum Disorder." *Journal of Autism and Developmental Disorders* 43:1539–1546.

Wheeler, E. A. 2013. "No Monsters in This Fairy Tale: *Wonder* and the New Children's Literature." *Children's Literature Association Quarterly* 38, no. 3:335–350.

Wielandt, T., K. McKenna, L. Tooth, and J. Strong. 2006. "Factors That Predict the Post-Discharge Use of Recommended Assistive Technology (AT)." *Disability and Rehabilitation: Assistive Technology* 1, no. 1–2:29–40.

Williams, C., B. Wright, G. Callaghan, and B. Coughlan. 2002. "Do Children with Autism Learn to Read More Readily by Computer Assisted

Instruction or Traditional Book Methods? A Pilot Study." *Autism* 6, no. 1:71–91.

Wilson, B. J., and A. J. Weiss. 1993. "The Effects of Sibling Coviewing on Preschoolers' Reactions to a Suspenseful Movie Scene." *Communication Research* 20, no. 2:214–248.

Winn, M. (Marcia). 1952. "Control Time Child Spends at the Television Set." *Chicago Daily Tribune*, April 3, C2.

Winn, M. (Marie). 1985. *The Plug-In Drug: Television, Children, and the Family*. New York: Penguin.

Winn, M. (Marie). 1987. *Unplugging the Plug-In Drug*. New York: Penguin.

Wong, M. E., and L. Cohen. 2011. "School, Family, and Other Influences on Assistive Technology Use: Access and Challenges for Students with Visual Impairment in Singapore." *British Journal of Visual Impairment* 29, no. 2:130–144.

Wright, C., M. L. Diener, L. Dunn, S. D. Wright, L. Linnell, K. Newbold, V. D'Astous, and D. Rafferty. 2011. "SketchUp™: A Technology Tool to Facilitate Intergenerational Family Relationships for Children with Autism Spectrum Disorders (ASD)." *Family and Consumer Sciences Research Journal* 40, no. 2:135–149.

"Youngsters 5 to 6 Give 4 Hours to TV." 1950. *New York Times*, April 11, 54.

Yuan, B., E. Folmer, and F. C. Harris Jr. 2011. "Game Accessibility: A Survey." *Universal Access in the Information Society* 10:81–100.

Zelizer, V. 1994. *Pricing the Priceless Child: The Changing Social Value of Children*. Princeton, NJ: Princeton University Press.

Zimmerman, F. J., and D. A. Christakis. 2007. "Associations between Content Types of Early Media Exposure and Subsequent Attentional Problems." *Pediatrics* 120, no. 5:986–992.

Zola, I. K. 1993. "Self, Identity and the Naming Question: Reflections on the Language of Disability." *Social Science and Medicine* 36, no. 2:167–173.

**The John D. and Catherine T. MacArthur Foundation Reports on Digital Media and Learning**

*We Used to Wait: Music Videos and Creative Literacy* by Rebecca Kinskey

*Quest to Learn: Developing the School for Digital Kids* by Katie Salen, Robert Torres, Loretta Wolozin, Rebecca Rufo-Tepper, and Arana Shapiro

*Measuring What Matters Most: Choice-Based Assessments for the Digital Age* by Daniel L. Schwartz and Dylan Arena

*Learning at Not-School? A Review of Study, Theory, and Advocacy for Education in Non-Formal Settings* by Julian Sefton-Green

*Measuring and Supporting Learning in Games: Stealth Assessment* by Valerie Shute and Matthew Ventura

*Participatory Politics: Next-Generation Tactics to Remake Public Spheres* by Elisabeth Soep

*Evaluation and Credentialing in Digital Music Communities: Benefits and Challenges for Learning and Assessment* by H. Cecilia Suhr

*The Future of the Curriculum: School Knowledge in the Digital Age* by Ben Williamson

For more information, see http://mitpress.mit.edu/books/series/john-d -and-catherine-t-macarthur-foundation-reports-digital-media-and -learning.